Finding the Divine:

A GLIMPSE INTO THE REALM OF GOD

Finding the Divine:

A GLIMPSE INTO THE REALM OF GOD

JANINE BOLON

The8Gates, LLC

2019

First Printing: 2019

ISBN 978-0-359-47864-4

The8Gates, LLC

1610 Pace Street, Suite 900, #225

Longmont, CO 80504

www.the8gates.com

Ordering Information:

Special discounts are available on quantity purchases by corporations, associations, educators, and others. For details, contact the publisher at the address listed above.

U.S. Trade Bookstores and Wholesalers: Please contact The8Gates, LLC, 1610 Pace Street, Suite 900, #225, Longmont, CO 80504

Tel: (720) 684-6535; or email Janine@the8gates.com

Testimonials

Janine Bolon's book *Finding the Divine: A Glimpse Into The Realm Of God* is a work of art. Janine takes you on a personal journey into a new world of possibilities that inspires, challenges your understanding of the universe and provides a process for exploring your personal concepts of reality. Without judgment or agenda, Janine gives you a glimpse into her personal story and an opportunity to embrace new questions that will lead you to a fuller life. Take a ride with Janine - you'll be glad you did. Enjoy!!

-Gary Barnes

International Speaker, Author & America's Traction Coach

Gary@GaryBarnesInternational.com

"With *Finding the Divine*, Janine Bolon offers a bold contribution to the long tradition of writings on the experience of spiritual discovery. Extremely personal yet utterly relatable and unpretentious, Bolon shares her insight into ditching expectations and releasing control in order to embrace pure potential and find joy. Stirring, genuine, and fun all at once, this book is a reminder that spiritual communication is in fact two-way and that everyone's personal Divine is out there with answers to all of our serious (and seriously pesky) universal questions."

-Steven Boyer, Utah

As I opened the book, I couldn't put down the book. It not only covers & brings clarity to so many questions I have had about God and Evil, Life and Death, Heaven and Hell and what happened after crossing over. But it is also a confirmation of what I have been studying till now. It is an easy and smooth read. It is so comforting to hear one more time EVERYTHING is divine plan with unconditional love, even death. It is an empowering to know even hell is our own choice. I am so looking forward to what Janine has to say in the next book!

-Sophia K., Texas

I have known Janine for a good, long time. She posses many special gifts. She has the innate ability to perceive what matters, in a spiritual sense. she has a wonderful sense of humor. This, combined with her willingness to be a conduit for spiritual light brings true joy to the process of learning. this newest book has only strengthened my feelings in this matter. I know I am blessed to be reading this book. So will anyone who reads this book with an open mind and an open heart.

-Gene O'Neill, Musician & Artist, North Carolina

I found this book fascinating. Not only were the stories and flashbacks intriguing, but many of the experiences Janine wrote in elaborate detail rang the bells of recognition for me. I knew, of the places she described, and I know what she wrote to be truth. I must admit that there was a tinge of jealousy because of how clear her memories are when mine are only clear when reminded by something, like the words she wrote. I thoroughly enjoyed this book, and I hope that others will receive the learning, understanding and joy in reading her words that I did.

-Brenda Hardwick; Author, Speaker & Healer

Here is your personal tour of the Astral Realms, Hell, the Akashic Records and other galactic frontiers. The journey that you will share with Janine, Jesus, Yogananda, the Devil, and Archangel Michael will captured your heart, your mind and your complete attention. Wonder no more what is in store for you now and what is waiting for you on the other side. If you are ready, she is here to guide you to your heart's desire.

-Trevor Mickelson
Senior Vice President, Speaker, Trainer
Living Benefits Specialist

"What are you looking for? The meaning of Life? Check. Adventure? Check. Learning what and who you really are to better know and understand yourself, the universe; the Divine? Check, check, check! Janine Bolon's "Finding the Divine: A Glimpse into the Realm of God" is an intimate, revealing—and often humorous!—telling of one divine soul's journey of discovering Truth and enlightenment, exemplifying that everyone of us is designed and fully capable of enlightenment also: Knowing fully who we really are, our Source/Infinite Love and embodying and expressing That Which We Are in this 3D reality. The reminders I got were profound as I laughed and cried in recognition reading Janine's book—being reminded of my whole being, my potential, my Source, my life's purpose and meaning (and my sanity!). This book reminded me about living my Truth, further developing my conscious partnership with Source, and validating my spiritual perceptions. For me, as a budding mystic with many of my own questions, this book is a guide I will come back to again and again to remind myself: I am Infinite and Divine Love in embodiment. The meaning and foundation of life is Love, which is All There Is. This human experience is meant to be a joyous adventure, and I get to choose my experience of life. Judgement isn't God's job. It's apparently ours. We are totally and absolutely loved. Love/God is the One and True Power. 'Evil' written backwards is 'live' and 'evil' is trying to live in reverse and serves the Divine plan as contrast for our experiences. Truly living is being in alignment and integrity with Truth/God/Love. "I exist, I am worthy and I AM Home. Thank You, God." I think this book is an excellent guide for mystics to remember who we are and why we came here in the first place. Janine's book takes you on a walk with your inner knowing and encourages you to discover that the answers you seek are are already within you to experience your most amazing life!

-Xochitl Ambrow
Soul Adventurer

Dedication

To my students, it only took a decade or so, but here's the book.

Thank you for your support and patience.

Mystic

noun

a person who seeks by contemplation unity with or absorption into the Deity or Source, and who knows of the spiritual apprehension of truths that are beyond the intellect.

-Janine's personal definition, 2010

***

"involving or having the nature of an individual's direct subjective communion with God or ultimate reality"

"having a spiritual meaning or reality that is neither apparent to the senses nor obvious to the intelligence"

- Merriam-Webster, 2019

Contents

Foreward

Few books leave me with tears streaming down my face. First caveat: I have read a lot of books in my life, so my statement about Janine Bolon's book, *Finding the Divine*, is significant. Second caveat: I personally know Janine, though not well in this life/timeline, but I Know her from what I call Home, that eternal Now Place which is also Here Now. Third caveat: I am the kind of reader Janine knows to be her audience. Spoiler Alert: She doesn't reveal that exactly, until the end.

As a scientist, mystic, healer, shamanic practitioner and self-ordained agent of transformation, I read Janine's book eagerly and with great interest, comparing notes, as it were. Although my experiences have been largely less "Technicolor" than hers, I've come to similar conclusions about what we human beings are up to here on the planet and what we're usually up to when we're not here in these "sacks of bones." It's both reaffirming and refreshing to find another mystic/awakened soul both in the service of All-That-Is and truly willing to tell the world about it, no sugar-coating added.

One of the concerns we might share when we occupy ourselves as both scientists and mystics is that the very society we assist may also consider us "crazy" for keeping one foot in the familiar material world and one in the Unseen, euphemistically speaking. Simply remembering who we *are* is a task that we may intuit but still require many years and experiences to accomplish. Living in a culture that paints the highest truths we know as "hogwash" can end with us as the stuffing for padded cells. Publishing a book along these lines is where only the intrepid tread.

In light of the foregoing risks, I applaud Janine's candor and courage in putting out her spiritual laundry for all the world to see. Her service to us in this regard is exemplary the way her spiritual laundry brings up the stains on our own egoic coverings in lovingly compassionate, benevolent and humorous ways. Through Janine's narrative, I see myself, my journey, and my own struggles with maintaining a strong connection with Home when the mud, tears and blood of human experience have splattered in my own life.

The Myth of Separation that is at the root of all our fears, anger and pain is both a societal and a deeply personal spiritual illness. To be honest, Janine's unflagging commitment to two-way communication with the Most High and her detail-oriented, wide-ranging scholarly search for the Meaning of Life, the Universe and Everything leave me feeling a little exhausted in comparison. I've been admittedly less ambitious, in my own view of myself, although I know some of my friends would disagree. My own approach has been intuitively synergistic, looking at the universals of culture and human experience. Yet, as a scholar myself, I know how much work it is to delve deep into the specifics of study, and I have a deep respect for Janine because I can imagine how many hours she faithfully has kept to the task of deeper inquiry. I am grateful to benefit from the results of her drive and determination.

You may be wondering then, why the tears? There were two places in her book where they fell and did not stop for long moments.

In the first place, I resonated with the White Space where she has kept connected with Daddy (her name for God) and had to acknowledge my own longing to be back Home, one with the One and All That Is, away from the recent years of pain here on this plane. Despite my Knowing that Home is as close as a breath away, I have felt bereft at times, all too "at one" with the world of appearances. I cried because I knew it was true when I read Daddy's reply to her, "You are in both places at once. Your consciousness resides in all places at once. You choose to focus on this life and now." I cried because I had to admit to myself how much I've missed that connection when I've wallowed in my own pain, grief, loss or anger. In taking my "this world" experiences so seriously, as if they were all that mattered, I've neglected the life long connection to my Source and All-Support. In that moment, at first I cried because I just wanted to go Home and be done with the hard work of being here. Then the tears fell because I knew that I was the one making the work hard by denying myself the support of that connection. My bad.

In the second place, I can no longer pinpoint exactly where the tears did flow or what exactly prompted them. However, I do know they were tears of recognition and resonance. I remember reading through her experiences of being called into awareness of being an awakened one. I never had anyone that I recall tell me exactly that I was awakened or enlightened.

However, I do remember distinctly a couple of experiences similar to two of hers. As a young early-twenty-something, I had three days of being in a state of oneness and bliss and feeling texture and temperature through my eyes, the same kind of synesthesia she describes. Ever since then, I have Known that I am one with everything despite putting that Knowing on the back burner in the middle of certain dramas in my life.

In the other experience, my then teenage daughter and I had a very much awake and aware conversation with the Presences of both Jesus and the Buddha, in which we both perceived and participated in the same conversation together. It's hard to deny Non-Ordinary Reality when it's simultaneously experienced and confirmed with another person you trust. You may read about that conversation and other experiences one day, as I will write my own story to add to the body of Knowledge. I thank Janine for writing hers first. I feel encouraged in getting mine written now.

What a relief to be "in" on the story of Evil and the tour of Hell! My teachers and my own mystical experiences had made it clear to me that there is only One Power and One Presence that counts, that evil is not to be feared, and that everything works to our good. Imagine my delight when the costume was unzipped and out popped... Well, that would spoil the story, so I won't go there! Suffice it to say that it's good to have one's own explanations of reality so thoroughly vindicated.

Another vindication of sorts is Janine's emphatic instructions on meditation and the importance of mystics, healers and shamans getting help from other mystics, healers and shamans. Her instructions are timely for all of us here doing the work of coaxing this world into an awakened state. Both Janine and Robert Burns, the Scottish poet, (read "To a Louse") really have it right. We have such a hard time seeing our own blind spots despite being adept at seeing those of others. I admit I have not been as consistent with my meditation practice, although I regularly recommend it to my clients. However, both Janine and I are right (and don't we all love being right!): all of us mystics, healers, and shamans benefit from the daily practice of meditation and time to reconnect with Source. I appreciate her reminders and recommend her classes!

Lastly, I want to remark on Janine's insightful summary of the major thought/belief errors that stymied her joyful and enthusiastic participation in the game of life that she selected for herself as an incarnate divine human. These are the very kinds of errors I work on with my clients to eradicate. Yet, as Janine herself also tells it, it's no small task to eliminate such errors from our own minds. Just since reading her book, I've accelerated my work on these kinds of errors in my own energetic field. Clearing them and replacing them with Truth takes courage, perseverance and a willingness to admit that we just might be wrong about ourselves, Life, the Universe and Everything. When it comes to the limitations we have placed on our perceptions of what is Real and What Is Not, there is no limit to our human imaginings of our separation from Source. A right use of our imagination is the weeding out of those limiting beliefs. Janine's short account of her own work on herself is a very useful guide for where we may find similar limiting, erroneous beliefs in ourselves that want uprooting and replacing.

By now, you can probably tell that I enthusiastically recommend Janine Bolon's new book, *Finding the Divine.* Once you read it and get on her mailing list, you'll probably find me among the first in line for her sequel, *Expressing the Divine.* And maybe you, too, will be inspired to write your own story of enlightenment, for your own benefit and for those who surround you.

-Jacqueline T. Ambrow, C.Ht., M.A.

Transformational Anthropologist, EFT Practitioner, Certified
Hypnotherapist, Musician
TransformationRoadtrip.com

Acknowledgements

◆

A s an author I've always found it difficult to put only my name on a book cover. There are so many people that help me in bringing my fledgling ideas into full flight. Especially on this particular volume, where it wasn't me sitting alone day after day creating the work you now read. A group of beta readers volunteered their time and energy to read every chapter (talk about keeping the pressure on to keep the chapters flowing). They walked along my storytelling road informing me of broken sentences, potholes of descriptions, and clashing inconsistencies from one chapter to another.

These beta readers are the true heroes of this book because they willingly trudged along the book-writing path that involved a mountain of chapters. It was slow slogging on some days when the trail was obscured by my all too abundant use of metaphors, commas, and sentence fragments. My hat is off to these wily adventurers; I couldn't have made my deadlines without you, Amber Mitchell, Amy Reese, Becky Lee, Bonnie Thompson, Brenda Hardwick, Gene O'Neill, Lisa Bernauer, Melissa Loresto and Patty Peritz.

A big thank you goes out to my editor, Barbra Rodriguez for her patience, guidance, and use of the red pen to make this book easier to read. Jabriellá Krown spent hours poring over text to copy edit this work. Please know any errors you find in this book are mine, not theirs.

Lastly, thank you to my children: Sean, Beth, James and Clare, who cleaned the house, made meals, and ran errands as I readied this manuscript for press. It truly takes a village to raise a child, no less so for an author writing a book.

Preface

W hat you are in the eyes of God is unlike anything you've been taught, especially if you're a recovering Catholic like me. I was six years old when my mom got cancer. She died fifteen years later at the age of forty-seven after three major surgeries, two rounds of chemotherapy and innumerable doctors' visits. Watching her illness and suffering was a contradiction to the God I had been taught about in Sunday School. How could God allow such a wonderful woman to suffer so horribly?

I wanted answers and I wanted them now! I wanted to talk to God, face-to-face. After traveling the globe, learning to meditate in three different religions and practicing as a mystic for twenty-five years, God did speak to me in 2010. This is a love story that took a quarter of a century to mature and retells the cuss-out sessions, experiences, and revelations delivered to a stubborn Fool (that would be me) from her loving God.

Did I mention cussing? Yes, one of the surprises ahead may be that God was fine with these expressions of true feelings as I sought greater spiritual understanding. I also cover my journeys to realms of heaven and hell, revealing unexpected ways that beliefs shape our afterlife experiences.

This book is rather autobiographical due to the insistence of my students. They have been asking me to write it for over a decade, and I'm now in a place where I can actually put words to the page. It is my purpose to show you how you can change if you want to and how you can live happily. I show through my personal experiences that you can connect to your version of the Divine person you want to be rather than remaining stuck as the type of person everyone expects you to be.

As for me, I was expected to stick to doing science, but began studying the lives of mystics while serving as a research biochemist back in the 1980s. Colleagues expected me to continue to work for pharmaceutical companies in the '90s, but I became a full-time mom with a passion for exploring the spiritual side of life, instead.

Although I've been able to see the spirits of animals, plants, and more for much of my life, my path as a mystic began in earnest in the late '80s, after reading the autobiography of Paramahansa Yogananda. In the past decade, I began working with Native American tribes on healing wounded spiritual places; soon after, the work expanded to using shamanistic experiences to help people heal spiritually as I connected to their departed loved ones, to their Higher Selves, or helped kick start their spiritual development in other ways. The path I took, which involved surrendering most expectations of what my life would focus on, has led to my development as a spiritual healer.

In this role as a spiritual physician, I have worked with Native American tribes from sixteen nations, as well as with everyone from Christian Deacons to Voodoo Priestesses. My hope is that what I have found after decades of seeking God and my personal growth as a mystic, you will be inspired to open up the doorway to your own unique spiritual understanding of the world, and ultimately, to the gift of remembering who you really are.

At the back of this book you will find a glossary and bibliography. Both are to help you with understanding different spiritual perspectives as well as provide you with additional resources for your life path.

When you're done reading this book, I would enjoy getting an email from you, where you describe your own personal experiences. I would be honored if you would teach me your stories.

Send me a note at Janine@the8gates.com. This way we, together as a community, can help others live the joy-filled adventure that they deserve.

-J.B.

July 2019

Chapter 1:
Seeking Romance

For most of my life, all I have ever desired was two-way communication with God. My first memory of this desire started when I was eight years old. I was sitting in my Sunday School class, bored out of my mind and feeling restless, when the teacher asked us, "Does anyone here know what the Ten Commandments are?" All the children raised their hands except me. I had no idea what the lady in front of us was talking about. I knew the story of Moses, but I never associated the words the "Ten Commandments" with Moses because I wouldn't see Charlton Heston in a movie of the same name until I was ten. It would be then that my overactive brain would connect the dots to the religious icon and his hike to chat with God.

I didn't understand what the Ten Commandments had to do with the love of God. I saw them more as the product of loving God. I was confused and I found it all so terribly, mind-numbingly dull. As a military kid living on a gorgeous Caribbean island, all I wanted was to go outside and play. When I was outside and smelling the ocean breeze, feeling the salt spray splash my face and the wind tussle my hair, I knew God in those moments. I knew He was playing with me and loving me in those moments, but I didn't know what an Angry God was all about. That God was very confusing to me. I didn't understand how the God who loved me was also the God who sent plagues, curses, and awful acts to His children. Wasn't He more like my mom? Didn't He love all of us like my mom did?

That memory of a long-ago Sunday School class on Eleuthera Island in the middle of the Caribbean Sea was the beginning of my search for God. He and I needed to have a heart-to-heart chat. I was even okay with having to climb a mountain by myself and listen to a pillar of fire, if that was what it took to get an audience with Him. Over the course of my life, I would see how different people worship their God as I traveled the globe with my family. Dad was in the Navy and we were able to move with him on several of his assignments to Japan and other places. I loved the experiences and found the different perspectives on life, culture and traditions refreshing to my active mind. I was enthusiastic with my learning, but quickly bored of a topic once I had managed to grasp the material. I wanted to move on to te next topic and not sit there doing worksheets over and over to prove that I knew what I had learned.

Instead, I would daydream and drum my pencil on my desk until my teacher told me to stop. By drumming my fingers under my desk, quietly, so my teacher wouldn't rebuke me, I was able to stay seated for the long hours of school. This activity kept me calm while I would stare out the windows, desiring nothing more than to play outside.

When we returned to America in 1977, my dad retired from military life. I was fourteen years old and the shock of American culture was huge. The pace of life was nothing like my upbringing. Americans were very informal and didn't seem to have the structure of the other societies I had been exposed to. My parents had moved us to a small town in southern Missouri. We were ten miles north of the Arkansas border and smack in the middle of the Bible Belt of the Midwest. I had never been in a more alien culture than living out my high school years in the Ozark foothills of Ripley County.

As a military brat, I had learned throughout my young life to "bloom where I was planted." After all, the brat's flower was the dandelion. Now, allow me to deviate a moment and explain what a military brat is. The term "brat" was one of many words commonly used in my family and by other military that was a positive, affectionate term despite the pejorative association many civilians have. Being a military brat is the oldest and most invisible American subculture there is. Pat Conroy, a military brat author, wrote, "We spent our entire childhoods in the service of our country, and no one ever knew we were there." Both my sister and I have been presented with military brat medals from our dad. It was amazing the honor and respect I have for both of my parents as we moved about the world and learned to adjust to all the different situations our family was thrown into.

My first semester of my freshman year of college, I was approached by two military men. It was 1982 and I had just walked out of my first college-level exam, with my head still spinning from the differences in testing methods and styles. I was walking amidst the throng of hundreds of students spilling out of the auditorium, fleeing for freedom on a warm summer day in Missouri. Two formal uniforms of the United States Marines were standing at the edge of the throng and I heard, "Janine Dalziel? A word, please." The "please" was not a civilian one. I could tell that I was being addressed in a military manner and despite the last five years of civilian life, my childhood training had me walking over to the marines before I knew what I was doing. I was shocked by my unconscious reaction. I shouldn't have been, but I was. I stood before these two men and said, "May I help you?" They smiled kindly and asked if I would be willing to let the military pay for my education by joining the Reserve Officer's Training Corps (ROTC).

First of all, I was stunned by the fact that they had pronounced my name correctly. Nobody ever pronounced my maiden name, Dalziel, right on the first go. Secondly, I was trying to figure out what they wanted. Once I understood they wanted me to serve in the military just like my dad had done, all became clear. I was invited to a meeting and I went. Why? Just to see what I could see. One of my desires while growing up in the U.S. Navy was being a helicopter pilot. I had wanted to fly those big banana boats, the Chinooks, or CH-47s. They are the heavy-lifting, twin-rotor helos. While I was in school, I'd hear those babies flying over and I would dream of one day flying in formation with them.

However, that dream would not manifest. It came up while I was in the ROTC meeting that if you had glasses, you were not allowed to become a military pilot of any kind. My dreams dashed, I went back to classes without signing up.

Being raised military, you learn to find joy wherever you are stationed. Otherwise, you'll be miserable for your entire tour of duty and find it hard to make friends. For my part, I learned early on that I liked people of all kinds and found them to be of the same basic mix no matter what culture, language or worldview they had. All the families I ever met, regardless of nationality, wanted the same things: a safe place to raise their children, their children's lives to be better than their own, and enough food to keep their family fed. Those common threads applied across borders.

Because that uniting thread was obvious to me while growing up in the Bahamas and other places, I didn't understand the racism that I found as we created a life and home in southern Missouri. It was hard being a gypsy traveler and finding such strong hatred based upon something as silly as skin color. It was in such strong violation of all that I had experienced up to this point that my mind revolted at the current culture I was in. I decided to finish high school quickly and get to college as fast as possible so I could start living again.

My family was fortunate to be surrounded by a network of friends that were also transplants to Ripley County. No matter where you go, you will find some military. And where you find military, you find friendship. The longer we lived in Ripley County, the more transplants we seemed to collect as friends. They were a delight and brought laugher, joy and excitement to our farm life.

Despite all the changes of culture, social mores and school, my heart still yearned for God. I found the local Catholic Church and started attending every week. The Catholicism practiced in southern Missouri is quite different from the Catholicism practiced on the island of Eleuthera where I had received my confirmation. The Missouri form of Catholicism had music that was always played in three-quarter time.

When I first attended church there, I thought that someone had died as I listened to the opening hymn. I looked up from my songbook and turned to face the back of the church, expecting to see pallbearers walking down the aisle any minute. The dreadful organ music was sending deep, low pounding vibrational tones throughout my body. After several Sunday masses showing me that the slow dirge-like music was how this particular Catholic Church "celebrated" God, I knew something was terribly wrong. The pews were filled with sad, frown-faced church goers who seemed to keep their heads down in sinner shame while they were praying. I was confused.

What happened to the joy-filled God of my youth? Where was He? Why was the joy and excitement of life moved down into a pit of sin, fire, hell and damnation? This sort of God was confusing to me and I couldn't get my mind around this philosophy. My heart knew that this sort of understanding was one based in fear. I didn't fear God. I loved Him and I needed Him in my life to show me what my life meant. I wanted a romance with God, but I had no idea how to share this concept with the people around me.

I then started visiting many different churches. Anytime anyone asked me to attend his or her church, I went. I wanted to see what this form of American Christianity was all about. It was so very different from what I had seen and experienced in other countries. My Buddhist teachers in Japan back in the early '70s had shown me Christ as a Master Yogi of Divine Love. Jesus the Christ was a man who had received enlightenment at a young age with a spiritual dispensation to remind his Jewish brothers and sisters, along with the rest of the Roman world, that love is stronger than hate.

During my middle school years in the Bahamas, I received tutoring by Obeah priestesses and Catholic nuns. I learned the ways of the tides, moon cycles, wind, and Christ's love for all humanity. I learned "to make a joyful noise unto the Lord," as the Bible puts it, by singing myself hoarse during mass while we laughed, clapped and danced in the aisles of the church celebrating Life. Then, after church, we would all eat conch fritters and have breakfast out on the beach near sandpits where food was being cooked in huge banana leaves.

However, the Christ I was learning about in the Midwest was a very different version. I learned that most Christians saw themselves as sinners and that Christ had saved them from dire death and destruction by dying on the cross for us. This was so alien to the Christ I knew that my heart revolted.

My Christ was a joy-filled, singing, laughing, and dancing kind of dude. Where was *that* guy? I couldn't find him. So, my search for a direct connection with God began in earnest. Where do you go when you're trying to find a man? You go to his wife, sister or mom. So, back to the Catholic

Church I went. I spent one Saturday afternoon in early May on my knees with Mother Mary, asking her to help me find her Son. I wanted to find the fun-loving Christ of my youth. He was the one I had heard laughing as the beach waves tickled my ankles and who danced with me in the sea foam. Where was He? I knew His momma would help me. And she did; it would just take a few decades.

Chapter 2:
The Angel's Bell

◆

I remember the night I really screamed at God. I mean, really had a bitch fest with massive cussing that would have made a sailor blush from my verbal takedown. I was in my last year of college in 1987, with finals coming up in a week for my degree in plant biochemistry. That's when I got the call that my mom had died. Her death had been a painfully slow one despite her fire and zest for life. Now, her flame was no longer burning. My immediate feelings after hanging up the phone were those of relief and happiness.

There wasn't going to be the frequent six-hour drives home every other weekend wondering if this would be the *last* time, I saw her. The past few years of her life had been a roller coaster of surgeries, chemotherapy and watching my mother's body slowly collapse inward. The medical treatments and bone cancer kept deforming her once vibrant body into a bald, skin-stretched-thin, skeleton-like frame.

She was now gone. I was numb for a moment before a wave of relief hit me, quickly followed by a huge blast of guilt that she had died, and I was happy about it. Her funeral was going to be this coming weekend and I would have to drive home to attend before taking finals during my last year in college. Here I was at age twenty-two standing in my dorm room feeling lost at sea. So, I did what I had always done. When alone, confused and uncertain, I dropped to my knees and prayed.

I was mentally challenging God to tell me what this *&%# life was all about; if this beautiful soul was dead, what did it all mean? I was kneeling by my bed with rage pumping through my veins. I was livid with Him and found that I couldn't focus on my studies. I knew my graduation was at risk due to some low grades and my frequent trips home. My roommate said it best when I was going home for the fourth time in as many weeks, "How do you deal with the death of a mom? A person who has been with you your entire life?" She had posed this question to me when I learned my mom's time was getting shorter. Her question focused my mind into that laser-like thinking I frequently have. She was right. How do we deal with the loss of someone that has been in our lives from the beginning?

As I knelt before God going over the prayers the priests had taught me during Catechism, my level of frustration, guilt and sadness sky-rocketed through me and I started to yell at God. I didn't cry. I had been taught from a young age not to cry and to always show strength not weakness when dealing with uncomfortable or terrifying situations. I was most definitely *not* going to be crying in front of my God. What I *was* doing was demanding some g#dd@m! answers.

In my training as a biochemist, I had been taught effective analytical reasoning skills and spent inordinate amounts of time in the library. My mom had spiritual gifts, and also taught me to see God as The Man that had *all* the answers. So, the practical part of me knelt in front of my mother's picture that I had encircled with black fabric, and I called out to God in a tone that was not humble, not cowering, not apologetic, but more a determined, "What the #@$% is going on?" I demanded He tell me why my mom's death had to be so awful, why she had to die so young, why He allows such awful things to happen to good people—and what is this Life stuff all about because I couldn't figure it out!

I was so intent on getting answers from God that my words galvanized into iron as I thought them. And I projected those heavy, metallic words straight to God Himself. I knew He could hear me. I demanded He hear me, and I was using those iron-infused words to push my way into His presence.

I felt a strange new strength of purpose flood over my being that I hadn't felt before as I said, "Amen." While I began to stand up, the weirdest thing occurred.

I heard a bell.

Not a bell like in church steeples or a tinny hand bell used to signal dinner, nor like a ship's bell when you're at sea. No, this bell was the highest, purest bell tone I had ever heard. I would refer to it later in life as the Angel's bell; what angel, I didn't care about, but I cared that God had heard my prayer and an angel of some kind had sent me a reply. The thought popped into my head, "message received." Wow.

I brushed away my tears. Wait, how did that happen? I didn't remember crying. Something had happened with time, because I thought I had been praying for only a few minutes, but a nearby clock suggested an hour had gone by. I noticed that my knees were numb from supporting my weight as I stood up and smoothed out the wrinkles of my nightdress. I climbed into bed emotionally exhausted, physically heavy, but spiritually satisfied that my world was in ruins, my future uncertain, but somewhere in the spiritual realm, my demand for answers from God had been heard. There was no flash of light, no angel chatting with me, no pillar of fire, just a single tone with "message received" in my mind. I knew God had heard me. Well, that was good enough to help me go on living for another day.

Chapter 3:

The Second Coming of Christ

◆

Fast-forward twenty-three years to the year 2010. Christmas was now rolling in and decorations had been set up, with music spilling out of many an electrical device reminding me of joys of the season. Brad and I had been married for over twenty years. We had four children and lived in Northern Colorado. Brad is a veterinary pathologist who travels as a consultant, and I was teaching classes and homeschooling all our children. We had wanted to live in Colorado our entire marriage and had just moved into our home the previous year. I was thoroughly enjoying having a first Christmas in Colorado.

As my family's activities of cookie baking, caroling, wrapping presents and gift anticipation increased that December, so did my joy. This time of year was always one that I relished. I cherished all the activities that were involved in the holiday. I know many folks view Christmas with a jaundiced eye due to commercialism, but for me, I still view it through the eyes of my inner child.

I love the lights, smells, sounds and excitement of the holiday. The sneaking around required so I could bring gifts into the house without the kids' knowledge. Finding hiding places so active minds wouldn't discover Santa's prizes, wrapping them and thinking of the happiness that follows, The joy of the entire day would always send me into such delight. I loved all of it.

My Jewish friends were teaching me about Hanukkah, and I was making many a mistake on the spellings, pronunciations and understandings of this Festival of Lights, but they knew I was in earnest to learn their customs and laughed off my attempts to wrap my tongue around some of the words. I was invited to several feasts and ceremonies and couldn't help but start humming each time the rabbi prayed. As the prayers were sung, I would feel myself get lost in the words, my body would gently rock side to side and my spirit would soar.

Christmas Eve that year was punctuated with an evening spent with my husband in a quiet house. We sat together in the living room with all the lights off except those of the Christmas tree. We were drinking hot cocoa and stirring our mugs with peppermint sticks.

Our tradition for many years was to put the kids to bed and, while they kept one another awake in their excitement, we would enjoy ourselves by listening to Patrick Stewart's one-man performance of *A Christmas Carol*. We had the cassette tape series and would pull out our old stereo player that was buried in a distant closet, dust it off and play the tapes on this "dinosaur technology." This year was no different. As we sat on the couch together, listening to Patrick Stewart and enjoying the peace of our home, I leaned into my husband's arm feeling the warmth and quiet joy of the moment. My heart was full and content. My soul sang songs of peace to the Earth. I wanted everyone to have a moment like I was having right now. I knew people would be celebrating in their own way, but I really wished deep down that every person on the planet could feel the peace and calm of the moment I was in. I closed my eyes like a five-year-old and silently asked God to find a way to make it so and if it wasn't possible, to at least have the courtesy to show me why. Little did I know in less than a week, God would grant this wish and many, many more.

***

A few days later I could hear the kids in their upstairs room happily playing with all their new loot. Brad had returned to work and I was sitting in our front living room reading a book. I was marveling at how long it had been since I was able to sit alone in a room without anyone needing me to hop up and get something. I cherished my reading time, which usually came at 3:30 a.m., when I could get some mommy "quiet time." However, here I sat in broad daylight, sipping a cup of coffee, eating some Christmas strudel, and reading a book. It truly was a magical moment for me. As I marveled at this event, I inwardly thanked God for gifting me this time and went back to the pages of *A Course in Miracles*. As I flipped through the book looking for a particular article, a sudden urge to look up came over me.

The wall of books across the living room from me wavered. I had seen something like this effect in movies when they were showing how spacetime would be in flux and you could see the fabric of our reality bubble or move. That was what was occurring in front of me despite being wide awake. I blinked. The wall was still warping. I closed my eyes again and shook my head. This time when I opened my eyes, I saw bubbles the size of sofas moving under the wall. I blinked my eyes rapidly and when I focused on the wall a third time, my body stiffened, and I froze.

There was no wall. Blinding white light poured out from the place where there should have been shelves of books. I watched Christ walk toward me from what appeared a great distance. This didn't make sense to my rational mind, nor did the fact that, as Christ came closer to me, he became more and more solid. It was like he was made of white wispy smoke and as he approached me, he became clearer to my vision and took on a three-dimensional (3-D) aspect. It is hard to relate this experience because the communication that followed between Christ and me was telepathic. There were a multitude of emotional undercurrents that went on with our discussion. Most people use voice inflection or facial expressions to convey their emotions. In this instance, any emotional tones that were needed for communication came into my heart and mind instantly, simultaneously. What Christ wanted me to feel, I felt in an instant. There was total and complete understanding.

The first thing that I noticed as Jesus the Christ walked and stood in front of me was his incredible eyes. His eyes carried all the Divine Love of the Universe within them. There was joy, laughter, humor, cleverness, hope, kindness, compassion, tenderness and a bit of a mischievous quality shining from his kaleidoscopic eyes. I could have stared at them forever and never become bored (*That* in itself is an unbelievable thing for yours truly!). His eyes were not any one color but all colors together. That's what it felt like as I gazed into them.

As I looked deeper into his eyes, I saw the Universe's creation, expansion and the evolution of the world, as we know it. Slowly my vision returned to the living room and Christ standing in front of me. He reached down and picked up my left hand. The entire time he was with me, I never felt the heart-racing excitement and curiosity that overcame me when I would see earthbound spirits, saints, demons, or angels.

Most of my life, I have been able to see the spirits of dead animals, people and plants. I was a clairvoyant as well as a clairaudient. This made growing up in a practical, military family a challenge. I had to learn what was considered "normal" in the eyes of other people and what wasn't. My mom would tutor me on what I could share with other folks and what I needed to keep to myself. It was because of my spiritual abilities and my deep desire to know how life works that I was driven to find God. I studied sacred texts of major religions, listened to hundreds of recordings and read dozens of books about the lives of mystics, shamans and saints. It was my avocation and one that I spoke about rarely. Being a scientist and a scholar allowed me to be quite methodical in my meditations and research on the Divine and, after daily meditations and thirty years of seeking God, Christ was now standing beside me in my *living room*.

As Christ gently held my hand in his, he said, "You are enlightened." This is the holy grail for a longtime seeker like myself. To be told that you have enlightenment means you have mastered your life and it is time for you to receive your spiritual dispensation (walking orders) and share them with the world. Yowzah. I felt like Christ had found the wrong person. How could this be possible? I knew I still had areas where I needed to grow as a human and was wholly unprepared and felt completely inadequate for the label of "enlightened person."

I was so befuddled by this experience that I actually turned in my chair *to look behind me* to see if he was talking to one of the kids who might have wandered by. I truly couldn't comprehend that *I* was the person he meant. So, here I was in the presence of the Divine. The main Man of God as far as Catholics and most Christians believe, and what do I say back to this Master of the Cosmos? How do I so brilliantly express myself to the Incarnation of Unconditional Love?

I looked up at him with child-like trust and said hesitantly, "Are you sure?"

I still laugh every time I recall this story. I just couldn't grasp that I had achieved this spiritual state. He looked down at me with such compassion. He repeated his statement to me with all the love and patience I have ever experienced all wrapped up in a huge gift of only three words, "You are enlightened."

I sat there trying to absorb all that this short sentence conveyed. The entire time I was processing this, Christ continues to hold my hand and I can feel his body heat as his fingers hold mine. I also started to realize I could feel calluses on his hands and that the longer he stood next to me the warmer I was getting, like the way you feel when you're standing next to your friend. You start to feel body heat.

Then out of the right side of my vision walks in Paramahansa Yogananda, who was the first enlightened one I followed as an adult. I normally would have dropped to my knees and honored my Guru, but instead I felt Christ's Love holding me in my seated position as my Hindu Master Teacher took my right hand and looked at me with deep intensity, saying, "You are enlightened." There I sat with two Masters of Life, Spirituality and the Universe, both telling me that I was enlightened. Eastern and Western spirituality were merging their metaphors, symbols, understandings and teachings in my heart and head.

I guess my mind finally decided to accept the fact because I heard an audible "click" sound in my head and I mentally said, "okay."

It was so crazy (mild understatement) to be sitting in my living room looking at the two men who had been my spiritual guides on Earth. I had been searching for decades for God - or as I like to call Him in my prayers, "Daddy." These two men had the same relationship with Daddy that I wanted and here they both were telling me that I now had that ability.

Christ then reached over, and I felt both of his large hands rest on my head. I could feel their heat and weight as energy coursed through my body down from my skull and into my bones all the way to my toes. After the blessing, Christ stood straight again and Guruji touched my third eye and a wave of blinding white light flashed into my head. As my vision cleared from the transmission of Light, Yogananda had left, but Christ remained. He was standing next to me, his hands at his sides.

Christ then spoke and gestured with his hand outlining a symbol in a way that I didn't understand at the time. I would see and hear this performed in a Jewish ceremony years later. "I give you the keys to the kingdom. You are a priest of my Father's house. All that I have you have."

Because of my many years of training in the schools of Catholicism, seven years of living in the rural south among Baptists, and many years of interacting with Mormons and their understandings of the priesthood, I, once again, demonstrated my incredible "intellect" to the Divine. I looked up at Christ in total seriousness and said, "You know I'm a woman, right?"

Why he didn't bust out laughing at me, I don't know. I laugh every time I think of this event and how silly I was/am in His presence. Instead, he just smiled down at me with his infinite patience, responding with humor in His voice, "I have a bit of a clue on that, yes." His smile got bigger and his beautiful eyes sparkled with delight. That he puts up with me shows his magnanimous nature.

My mind churned as I thought about the pushback, I would receive about being a High Priest with the keys of the Kingdom. As I thought about sharing this story, I saw lots of difficulties and resistance. I looked up at Christ and said, "This sure is going to piss off a lot of men." He nodded in reply, "I know. I still need you to accept the gifts given to you." My consciousness was then pulled out of my body as Christ took me to his "Father's house of many rooms."

As I'll describe later, I saw where we go when we die. I saw how various souls sort themselves into different regions of Creation. I saw that we are not judged upon death, but that we judge our own lives, and that our Creator stands beside us in whatever form we are most comfortable with; such as

Buddha, Krishna, Shiva, Vishnu, Christ, Muhammad, Solomon, Confucius, Moses, Divine Mother or a Heavenly Father, each will work with a soul during the transition to their next evolutionary experience after leaving the Earth plane. Whatever form or identity makes the soul the most at ease is the one presented at death to walk with the soul. It is the soul that looks over each life and decides how the most recent life experience has played out. The soul makes the judgments, not God. The soul made the decisions, not God.

I popped back into my physical body, where I was still seated in my living room in Colorado. I took a deep breath. I don't know how long I was gone, but I felt like I had traveled millions of miles and that it took hours. Christ was pulling his hand off my head when I came back into my body. I watched him retreating from me as he returned to his realm. I had received enlightenment and diksha. My world would be forever changed.

After Christ's departure, the first thing I remember doing was looking down at the book I had been reading, which was still open on my lap. I felt the weight of it on my thighs and I looked out the bay window of the living room and saw the sun shining brightly and beautifully through the glass. There was a prism-like quality to the window I hadn't noticed before and I was seeing layered rainbow-like effects playing all over the glass. I realized that something had happened to my vision. I was still seeing the world as I thought I should see it, but there now seemed to be some sort of overlay that was entering my mind as if I was seeing the light fracture and actively create the world.

I watched as Light manifested through the various energies as it created reality in real time. My mind watched as Light became thought. Thought became energy. Energy became mass. My mind then interpreted the signals my eyes received and added labels such as "tree," "stone," "street" and "window." As I continued to process what I could see, I had no idea how I would ever be able to communicate in words what had occurred to me. I held what had been shown to me in my heart. I was in awe. I sat in Bliss.

I don't know how long I was in that chair before I got up, but what I do remember is that one of my children hollered down to me asking if I would make some lunch and could it please be macaroni and cheese. I was grateful they wanted a simple meal. I didn't think that I could handle anything too complicated. As I prepared the ingredients for mac and cheese, I was having problems moving around in my body. I felt like I was using some lumbering vehicle that had sticky hydraulics. I wanted my arms and legs to move in a certain way and all my body would respond with was a bunch of bumbling about.

I took a deep breath. I started using the breathing techniques I had learned from Yogananda to settle my mind when emotionally upset. That helped a bit, but the challenge was I wasn't upset. I was in euphoria. I was in bliss. I loved everything and everyone. I was incapable in that moment of one negative thought or dark emotion. I was filled with Light and all I could see was the beauty, color and prism-dispersed Light everywhere that manifested into forms to create all that is upon this Earth and Life.

I dug out the pasta pot from the lower cupboard and put it under the faucet to fill it with water. I was struggling to keep my mind focused on feeding my children lunch. But now, when I looked out my windows to the yard, trees, bushes and rocks, I saw myriads of color combining and dancing. I have never taken LSD or any other recreational drug, but I was beginning to think that maybe this was the kind of experience a person had. I was staring in awe as I watched birds fly over the treetops and land on the higher branches. I was giggling as I saw squirrels gamboling about tree branches playing tag. I could hear their joy and felt their energy. I was in the branches playing with them while I stood holding a cooking pot under a stream of water.

I snapped out of focusing on the squirrels and birds when water started spilling out of the pot and splashed onto my shirt. I quickly reoriented myself and shut the water off. As I poured off the excess liquid and set the pot onto the stove, I could feel I was moving differently and sensing everything differently. I was seeing Life in a whole different way. As my kids came thundering down the stairs to find out when lunch would be ready, I asked them to set the table. I was busy getting ingredients out for the cheese sauce and I would need their help. As they grabbed various dishes, cups and silverware for the table, my mind and heart were busy taking in this common everyday sort of scene and I was seeing it and experiencing it with a new sense of wonder that left me almost breathless.

I saw patterns and swirls of electromagnetic energy and light all around my children. All I could do was stare at them as they moved about getting prepared for lunch. I don't remember much more about that day other than, I burned the mac and cheese onto the bottom of the pan, but not so much that most of the pasta couldn't be eaten. I eventually had to throw the blackened pan away.

I would discover over the next three days, I wasn't much good at cooking, teaching or doing much else other than conversation. Thank heavens it was the winter holiday break at school. I was spiritually walking worlds with Daddy's Masters. Christ wasn't done showing me his Father's House. He was about to take me on a tour. It would take three nights in a row. I would finally be able to sleep on the fourth day.

Chapter 4:
A Tour of Heaven

I struggled to sleep that night because of the pure energy coursing through my body. I suspect I drifted off around midnight, but I awoke at 2:30 a.m. and knew there was no way I was going to be able to sleep anymore. I got up, donned a robe over my pajamas and headed over to my meditation chair. As soon as I sat down, closed my eyes and focused my mind on my third eye, Christ was there, waiting for me.

This time he was not in the 3-D form. He was in the shamanistic world of the mystic. We were in the astral plane moving about that realm of Life. The astral plane is the first vibrational frequency that clairvoyants view. It is slightly higher than the Earth plane frequency. Psychics, mystics, and shamans see where souls go when they leave the body and frequently the astral plane is the middle ground used for communication between souls still in a body and souls no longer in a 3-D body. After Christ saw that I was fully present in the astral plane, he turned to move away and reached behind himself with his hand outstretched, clearly waiting for me to follow. I wasn't as efficient as some shamans about moving to the higher frequency states, but after a few minutes of calming my breath to the breathless state, I was able to follow him.

Instantly he took me to a gorgeous place of white tulips. We were walking toward a pure white gazebo that was made totally of marble. There was a comfortable-looking bench in it built for two. As we walked toward it,

I noticed there was something very odd about the field of flowers. At first, I wouldn't follow Christ because I didn't want to step on the gorgeous white tulips, but as we stepped toward them, they moved out of the way and created a small path for us to traverse.

As we moved through the sea of white tulips, I watched Christ's robe gently brushing the flowers and saw why they looked funny to me. They weren't tulips at all. They had tulip leaves and stems, but the flowers on top were roses. The plant biochemist in me stuttered. How was this possible? As soon as I had this thought, Christ leaned over and smelled a rose and looked at me and smiled. "I made this place for you. This is our special place. Come here whenever you like. It is yours." He held the rose between his thumb and forefinger so I could see its beautiful head. As the flower moved to his touch, I realized that he had planted this immense field with purpose. He had wanted me to remember something.

Early in my marriage I had placed a white rose at the feet of a statue of Mother Mary and I had asked that I be the best wife I could be to Brad, but that I would still have a spirituality that kept me strong as she had been. "That's right," confirmed Christ, "This is the one you gave my mother." I was speechless. The amount of emotion I had coursing through my being would have overwhelmed me had I been in my earthly body. But here I could transmute the power of any emotion (anger, hate, guilt, shame, surprise, etc.) into Love. I didn't need to break down into a weeping mass of tears and gratitude and understanding as I do when I type these experiences for you to read.

We walked on toward the gazebo where he sat down on the bench and motioned for me to sit next to him. The bench looked like pure, white marble with exquisitely carved filigree and symbols all around the sides and back, but when I sat upon it, the feeling was like a softly cushioned couch. The bench had gently received my form though the marble was cool to the touch. This inconsistency was matter of fact in the moment, but as I write about this event, my logical mind still rebels at how the "possibility" of these various discrepancies can coexist in a single moment. Welcome to the world of a mystic, folks.

As we sat on the bench together, I could tell that we were waiting on something or someone. I enjoyed the crisp smell of the flowers that didn't have any particular scent other than "fresh." There was a breeze gently blowing them back and forth and I waited, perfectly content to just sit with Christ in this place of beauty, peace and calm. Then I saw a flash of something in the distance. As the movement continued, I could tell it was a man moving toward us dressed in a robe of the same material and style as Christ was wearing. As "he" got nearer his features, coloring and clothing became more and more distinct. I realized from all my readings that it was Archangel Michael who had joined us, complete with his breastplate and spear. Christ turned to me and said, "I need you to do something for me. I would like you to tour the heavens with the angels. See what you can."

I spent the rest of the night touring the levels of heaven and learning from the angelic beings. I watched as people died and moved through the various regions of space as they matched their energy to the frequency of the region their soul needed to reside in for healing, comfort and Love. There was a hospital-like structure for people who had recently passed from earth. In that space they were laying in beds all cocooned up in blankets that were healing blankets. For those who had experienced rather traumatic, harsh lives, they needed more time in the healing blankets than those souls who had experienced deaths or lives that were less violent.

Those who, were in need of more Love than they got on Earth were given extra attention and compassion before they felt ready to leave. It was totally up to the individual soul as to when they would go or how long they would stay. I had seen this before in doing spiritual work with Native Americans. Some tribal members would be wrapped in their funeral blankets for three days before we shaman would be allowed to talk to them and to give their messages to the tribe, but this astral event was showing me the Christian perspective.

I walked among the rows and rows of souls in blankets as the spiritual caregivers moved about giving healing. I pondered whether, at some point, I could have seen Florence Nightingale in this place. It seemed exactly like the sort of hospital she had always wanted to create in her time. I was told by one of the caregivers that the soul I called Florence Nightingale was otherwise engaged at a different spiritual level. My heart was warmed by that news. My mom had been a wonderful nurse and cared for people on a very deep level. She used Florence Nightingale as a role model. The energy of this healing place reminded me so much of the "why" behind nurses giving their lives for their healing craft. Their desire to be in medicine came from a place like this.

I was then taken to a different region of heaven where I was introduced to a lady by the name of Ms. Nancy. She looked very much like a nun of the days of old and was in charge of taking care of the children who had died. Large groups of children were here playing. I sat with the kids and played for a long time (being such a kid at heart!). The children taught me why they stayed in this region of heaven rather than moving on to the other areas. They were present to help their families with the grieving process and to teach them the continuation of the soul.

I was invited to watch them as they interacted with their families on Earth. They could be seen comforting their moms, dads, siblings, and extended family. They knew the emotions of their families and friends and would appear in their dreams, visions and through music. I would see songs in church being sung that were the children's favorite. They would have songs play on the radio while the family drove to remind them of good times.

I was then asked to leave the children's area of heaven (sigh, I loved it there!) and head to where people were learning. It is difficult to describe this region, but I had read books that helped me with the necessary words for the different regions of this spiritual plane: *Life in the World Unseen*, by Anthony Borgia, and *Autobiography of a Yogi*, by Paramahansa Yogananda.

These books describe the experiences of individuals as they moved about the spiritual realms. Each book covers a different paradigm of how the soul realm looks based on the time period the visitor lived in, their cultural upbringing and life purpose. Because of the lessons each visitor needed to learn and bring back to humanity, each was given certain information they needed to share. For the work I've been called to do and the experiences I've been asked to share, I find both authors to be correct. I have experienced most of what they talked about, as well as having received added information from my own shamanistic experiences with Native Americans, and from the Japanese and Caribbean cultures I grew up in.

I think now is the time to give you a bit of background on what shamans, psychics, saints, and spiritual gurus experience as they move about the Divine Realms. Here is a brief tour of the basic levels. I encourage you to meditate and define for yourself what each level means for you as your soul continues moving through its adventure-filled evolution.

The first particular energetic frequency of the spiritual realms upon death or shamanistic journeying is referred to as the astral plane. The astral plane is a level of frequency visited by shamans from hundreds of different cultures all over the world who use the sixth sense to travel and gather information. It is a crowded frequency with lots of traffic and noise. Think of an AM station on the radio or browsing YouTube. In this realm there are many different souls moving about. Here you can think of anything and it will instantly materialize before you. You are able to create homes, gardens, libraries, and whatever other environments are to your liking. You have the ability to move about many regions in this frequency without difficulty. A soul can think and focus on anything and, ta-da! It will be created. It is here where some seers and psychics have described streets of gold and huge palaces and riches beyond imagining. Many souls work together to make up the creation of this realm. You will find all manner of artistic endeavor here. This is the realm young children remember with crystal clear clarity. It is this realm that makes them frustrated, that everything is so molasses slow on planet Earth, like the fact that we have to drive in cars rather than teleport. This makes some children extremely annoyed with the 3-D world.

If, as a soul, you express a desire to know more or learn more, it is instantly manifested, or you are taken to a region of this frequency that already has the information in place for you. Since I'm a scholar and teacher, I was shown entire cities of learning, libraries and hubs of knowledge. I was able to wander about a whole city that was one huge library, with each building in it representing the knowledge that a civilization had gained up to the present. I walked about inside several of these libraries that had scrolls, clay tablets, books, digital media and other compatible forms for my viewing. I quickly realized I could spend lifetimes here quite happily learning all that was available for a soul to learn. I thought about seeing how all this information was used and was immediately teleported to a stadium-like structure. Here teachers were lecturing to hundreds of thousands of souls about the various worlds in all of creation. These souls were preparing to live future incarnated lives and were learning about the type of areas they could inhabit.

No notes were being taken since all knowledge was easily accessible using telepathy. There was a beautiful light everywhere I went, and when I thought about the light and had a question in my mind about what a night in this place would look like, instantly I was teleported to a region of the astral plane that had night. Hundreds of souls were here studying the stars and the night "sky" with a multitude of instruments, conversing on the beginning of constellations and how stars are made throughout multiple universes. In essence, these souls were studying different universal creations.

I thought about being back in the amphitheater of classes and I was instantly there; but I wasn't in one of the seats this time, I was in the wings off the stage with another soul who was dressed as a monk. I couldn't tell what faith he represented, but I could feel that he was an advanced soul. He was there to guide me through the other realms of heaven. He told me he didn't often make it to this frequency because he was a teacher of the higher energetic levels of frequency. As we moved away from the teaching theater, I could feel us shifting into a different vibratory level.

I need to share something important about these levels. There is no judgment about levels of frequency. I am unable to stress this enough in my teaching classes and 1-to-1 coaching sessions. Each soul needs to move on their journey of creation differently. One level of frequency isn't performing better than another level. There is no hierarchical judgment to these frequencies. I like using the term "frequency" to explain the many areas of experience because of my scientific training.

When I was in the laboratory working on robotic arms and automated processing systems, we frequently employed an oscilloscope. I used this device almost daily to see the changes in electrical signal as a sample of blood or other substance was being processed and tested. We would measure the signal in the unit of volts, and the instrument continually graphed what was occurring over time with a calibrated scale. We would analyze the various waveforms we saw for the amplitude of their waves (how tall they were), their frequency (how short the time was from the top of one wave to the top of the wave that came along next) and for the distortion of the waveforms (change in a waveform from the original one observed). For my artistic and musical readers, oscilloscopes can measure sound forms and image forms, but in this laboratory setting, we dealt with electrical waveforms.

Ask a scientist, mathematician or musician, and you'll find that they have no judgment about experiencing a waveform as either a sine wave or a cosine wave. Sometimes a musician wants to create a distorted sound of a lower frequency as part of creating a certain tune. This sort of distortion is not seen as "bad" or "lower;" it is simply seen as a part of the song.

My purpose with the oscilloscopes was looking at the frequencies being generated by an electromagnetic field. I'd harmonize my instrument's recording of an event with the frequency being manifested by a control sample. I'd work the dials of the oscilloscope until the frequencies lined up, and then I'd know that I had achieved harmony to clearly capture the sample's true frequency.

I found the same sort of perspective being used in the different spaces of the metaphysical world. The difference was that Unconditional Love permeated every action, thought and intention. The only desire in the realms of spirit is that each soul be in the frequency that rendered the best harmonization for them so the soul could feel unity. That's the best way I know of to describe the many metaphysical regions and levels I have experienced.

My guide moved me into a region between two frequencies. I heard in my head "The space between the spaces," and all I could see was a fuzzy white space. It was blindingly white and indistinct (Like the first time I saw Christ walk through the wall of white light). I asked my guide about it and he said, "Oh that part of this realm hasn't been created yet. It is the space that allows each soul to create what it desires. If we have a space that fits a thought, people naturally move into it. However, if there is a customized feature that is needed or a new thought needing to be accommodated, this is where it is made. You are seeing pure potential thought here."

Whoa. It took me a minute to get around the enormity of what my guide just said. That statement would allow me to make some huge changes in my life and the lives of clients for the future. Note to self, "Don't forget about the power of pure potential."

I asked if I could ever see inside pure potential. He looked back at me and smiled. "You will be there soon." That made me happy and I went back to focusing on our travel into a new area of heaven. This section of frequency was less distinct than the astral plane. In this realm everyone was dressed exactly the same.

Here individuality was expressed through the vibrational frequency resulting from accumulated experiences of many lives lived in different worlds and realms, as well as the soul's frequency of occupation in this place. Here was a region of creation that required each occupant to have a strong discipline of the mind. Each thought merged with many others. If you had an undisciplined mind that wandered about unfocused, chaos would have been created here.

Any thoughts I was having were immediately picked up by the other souls around me and they were molding their own thoughts to mine while maintaining conversations and communications with those around them. There were many such conversations going on at once and it was like having eight regions of your brain activated simultaneously. Rather than trying to track everything that was going on in my brain, I allowed full access to anyone who needed it; within fifteen seconds, I felt a relaxation occur in my mind. For the first time in my memory of life, I had no barriers built up around my mind's thoughts. I allowed anyone and everyone to "talk" to me in any way necessary.

It was novel. And not as intrusive as I thought it would be. As soon as another soul started to flip through the memories in my mind to learn more about me, I could feel their love, and their gratitude for my experiences. They were happy I had lived whatever memory I had. They could create "better" because I had the memories I did. That was the difference. That's why there was never a judgment about things being "right" or "wrong" in a soul's journey. As each experience, memory and lesson of my soul's journey in my current life (as well as the many past lives I had lived) was made available to the other souls, no negativity was ever expressed by what they saw of my experiences. I was never judged. I was appreciated in ways we just don't experience here on Earth.

However, if a memory became uncomfortable for me, the soul looking into them would immediately stop and move to a more comfortable memory for me to share. It was done instantaneously because the love of this region was so strong it was the only emotion allowed in this space. Discomfort meant resistance, and nothing in this region was done with force. Ever.

Yogananda called this region the causal plane. I was now standing in a region of heaven where thoughts were created. I was seeing how thoughts were formed by souls and how they could manifest these thoughts at all levels of creation. This was the region of creation that started the process of moving light and love into an astral form. That was what I was thinking at the time. I would be shown later that this identification, or label, of this realm was incorrect. I was later shown that the causal plane had many more levels above it. Based on my spiritual education up to then, I had expected this realm to be only one step away from God Himself. However, I would be shown a different perspective over the next two days.

As I moved about this frequency, I met many guides, souls, teachers, and beings. All were my friends. Some I remembered, others I felt like I was meeting for the first time. For the souls that I didn't remember, my guide would explain my status. He would state that I was still in an earthly body and I was traveling around learning the place. There were many times I would have a soul approach and flip through my thoughts in my head. Because I was in memory of the year being 2010 on the "timeline" and that I had a female body on planet Earth and was living in North America, this unremembered friend/soul would think to my mind, "Ah, that's where you are. Okay. You and I are dear friends; come back when you remember-I can't wait to catch up!" It was so weird to hear this form of casual talk in my head after all the higher forms of conversation going on around me. I could feel that I was thinking from a perspective of separation in a way that these other souls were not experiencing. Wow. Total mind bender.

My guide turned toward me and said, "I will see you again soon." We embraced and all I could see around me was blinding white light. I wasn't in any way made uncomfortable by it, but my mind could not process a single thought. It was like I was frozen in time and all I could experience in that moment was light.

I was back in my body. The sun was up. I looked at the clock next to my meditation chair. It was 6:00 a.m. I felt like I had been gone days, not hours. The kids would be up and moving in a matter of moments. I needed to go be a mom now and get breakfast ready. I slowly stood up. It was going to take me twenty minutes before I felt comfortable being in my body. I felt like it was big and bulky. I was having difficulty working with it. My arms and legs felt like they were heavy balloons filled with concrete that were responding incredibly slowly to my thoughts. I suddenly realized. "Oh, right. I'm not in heaven anymore. Down here things vibrate slower and that means thoughts travel slower as well."

I managed to stumble into the shower. The hot water was tap dancing on top of my head which helped tremendously. By the time I was on my second cup of coffee, I was able to make breakfast. The day passed by with the hundreds of details running through my brain that each day requires when you're running a household, teaching classes and keeping children in a good place. That night would be something different.

Chapter 5:
A Tour of Hell

M y day was over, and I was preparing for another night of meditation and very little sleep. As I brushed my teeth and tried to process all the information I had received regarding heaven, I noticed how my entire body was energized even though I had had a full day of activities with the kids, errands and lots of phone calls to family and friends reconnecting during the holiday season. As I made sure the doors were all locked and the lights out, I wandered back into my meditation room, looking forward to what this evening's experiences might be.

My teachers and guides were waiting for me as soon as I finished my opening prayers and calmed my breath. The second I said, "Aho and Amen," I was pulled from my body and I was standing in the tulip-rose garden with Christ and Archangel Michael (AA Michael). I went down on one knee immediately before Christ on instinct. Both Christ and AA Michael pulled me up by my armpits with Christ pointedly saying, "We don't have time for this. We need your help." Me? Help? I couldn't fathom why these two amazingly powerful Masters would need me. A lot of telepathic information was passed among AA Michael, Christ and me. It seems AA Michael was reporting in about the state of affairs in some realm and they needed me to go retrieve some souls.

What?

Retrieve souls?

Wait a minute.

Before I could process this new data dump, Christ thanked AA Michael for his work and gently held my upper left arm as we began to descend in frequency. I got heavier and heavier and heavier. It was gross and I didn't like it. If I hadn't had Christ next to me, there is *no way* I would have ever traveled to these lower, sluggish realms. This frequency was dense.

Christ's robe went from being a beautiful snow white to rainbow iridescence to blinding white light that soon lost form around the edges and became fuzzy. It was like my eyes couldn't focus on where the robe ended, and the rest of reality started. As our frequency slowed, the environment around us became dense, thick and heavy. Oh, and did I mention dense? Think of being made of concrete and trying to move around in mud. Ugh! Colors were gone. The world around us was nothing but gray. The region we were descending into had a perpetual overcast gray look and the light here was muted and dull. The buildings, streets and other spaces were all monochrome. It was like we had entered a land that was labeled, "Depression." It was visually representing what a depressed person feels like. There were many different streets and buildings. They were all morphed together, and it was difficult for me to distinguish anything specific. So much of this realm was blurred, fuzzy and cloudy. Even the clouds had a gray hue. The only thing that burned with any color was Christ's robe. It still shimmered white, yet it, too, had lost all the iridescent qualities I had seen earlier.

We stopped in front of a door. He told me, "This soul has been here for over 300 years. It is time for him to leave this place. He needs to come home." I just nodded, because, honestly, I didn't know what else to do. Christ knocked on the door and I heard a quiet, masculine "come in." The voice even sounded withdrawn. Before Christ crossed the threshold, he looked down at his clothing for a moment and then made his robes the same color as the outside of the building. He looked at me and I heard in my mind, "You stay white." I looked down at myself. Wow! I was stunning. I was radiant. My robe was iridescent white and sparkling with rainbows of color. I could hear muted voices in the house, and I tried to walk into the room. But I felt gently stopped mid-step at the threshold, the frequency of the room wouldn't let me in.

The house was made up of one room. The walls looked to be made of gray mud and had been put together by one person. The ceiling had timbers laid across the top. Outside it had a gray grass roof. There were no windows in the single room. There was a fireplace, an old one like you see in frontier homes from the early 1800s. However, no fire burned on the grate and the kettle hook didn't have a pot for cooking.

I then saw the man. He was sitting at a rather forlorn-looking table that had two chairs, the one he was sitting in and the one holding Christ. I managed to finally move and step into the room, but I was taller than the ceiling and I had to duck down to keep my head from brushing the beams.

Christ was leaning on the table talking intently to the man as the man leaned back in his chair, his arms dangling limply at his sides listening. As I walked in, the man turned and looked at me and said, "My God, it's an angel!" "Yes," said Christ. "It is time for you to come home with us. This angel is here to guide you." The man stood up shakily and said, "But I've been bad, I don't deserve to be anywhere near people." Christ walked over and helped the man to his feet while steadying him. The man couldn't take his eyes off of me. He just kept staring and staring. Then a change started to occur. Slowly his face and skin turned from an ashen gray complexion to a hint of color. The energy that makes color was slowly moving around him. Color was coming back to his skin. He was slowly losing the gray look of a concrete statue and was remembering who he was.

Christ managed to gently move the man to the door as I backed out of it to let the two of them step across the threshold. As the man stepped outside, he dropped to his knees and started crying, he was talking so fast and mumbling something about wanting to go home but not deserving love or heaven. I realized that this man had kept himself in this place for centuries after his death because he felt that he didn't deserve God's love or love of any kind.

Nothing could be further from the truth. With all that I had seen and experienced of Love over the past few days, I knew for certain, he would be celebrated and cherished. I bent over to help him to his feet and noticed the huge wings on either side of me. The tips of feathers were brushing the ground as I leaned over to assist this soul. He looked up at me and said, "No, no you're too bright. You're too bright!" I quickly retreated and Christ came over and lifted the man to his feet. Christ was murmuring words of comfort and friendship to the man the entire time he helped him and walked with him. It was an amazing sight to behold. It took multiple tries, but the man got to his feet a second time. I noticed how the entire environment was lightening in color in response to the changing color of this man's skin. What I hadn't noticed before was this entire neighborhood was vacant. It now occurred to me that only this soul lived in this town. He had completely isolated himself.

Slowly the gray was being replaced with light. It was like the dust of the place was being removed and the fog of depression was lifting. The man was gaining more and more color as time passed. Christ then asked the man if he was ready to see his family. That they were waiting for him, I thought the man was going to break down into tears again, but he managed to receive this information and absorb it rather than be crushed by it. He was more incredulous than anything when he asked, "They're here? Waiting for me?" Christ told him we only had to think of loved ones, and they would be with us. In an instant all of us were in a fuzzy white space. The man was standing among a group of people. He saw his wife and friends. As they all smiled, greeted and embraced one another, Christ looked at me and we were immediately back in our tulip-rose garden sitting side-by-side in the gazebo on the loveseat.

"Wow, I got to be an angel. Thank you." I was laughing at the wings and the gown I was dressed in for the man's benefit. "Did I have a halo too?" I couldn't help laughing. I was so happy for the man and so grateful to have left the heaviness of his hell. My heart was skipping along merrily and was rejoicing in another soul being released from the darkness created by his own misunderstanding.

Christ was laughing along with me. His eyes were sparkling like diamonds and I was lost in their love and kaleidoscopic light. Everything was so amazingly beautiful and good in that moment. Christ went on to teach me how souls will create their own hells and, when they have been in those places for a certain amount of time, it is our job as mystics to go and find them and release them from their misunderstandings of how the Creator really loves.

As I looked out over the sea of tulip-roses, I noticed Grandfather of the West (see glossary) on the horizon, standing at the edge of the garden waiting for me. Christ said, "He needs to take you to other places and will train you on mass soul recovery." Christ was already starting to fade, and his form was slowly becoming more and more transparent as he finished talking. "There are three other levels I want you to visit. Some of those souls need to come home."

The love seat, gazebo, and tulip-roses faded from view and, magically, I was standing next to Grandfather of the West. As I continued to watch him, he slowly morphed into his Grim Reaper form. This "Father of Death" outfit was created and recognized across different religions, cultures and ages. Grandfather of the West or "Death" would morph and transform into any visual version of Death that was needed depending upon the understanding and cultural perception of the soul's most recent incarnation.

His current costume had a floor-length, hooded black robe where you couldn't see his face. I could feel him smiling despite the fact his face was just a skull. He allowed his emotions to be easily read by me. He had a long wooden staff that reached his shoulder that he used as a walking stick. About six inches from the top of the staff, an antique hourglass dangled that was attached with what looked like silver thread. I started laughing when I saw his costume and all the marvelous symbols that detailed not only his occupation, but quite literally, his role as *The* Keeper of Time. As he stood before me letting me inspect all that he was in that moment, I rushed forward and hugged him as hard as possible.

I finally had overcome forty years' worth of confusion. Death had been with me my whole life. I had seen him in so many different cultural metaphors that I hadn't strung them all together into the beautiful chain of Love that he represents until this very moment. He has been my unexpected guardian angel, and the more I learned about his many facets, the closer I was to God. His love for mankind was evident. He gave each soul as much time as he could. He never interrupted someone's life or journey until they (the soul) allowed it.

Literally, Death is the ultimate gentleman. He is civil, kind, respectful, but also obedient to each soul's timetable. When their time is up, Death arrives and reminds them of their next appointment on their soul's journey. It made me giggle even more as I thought about all that Death was and all that he embodied from this vast perspective of time, space, life and adventure.

The Grim Reaper, Grandfather of the West, or should I say, the Angel of Death in Christian vernacular, was taking me to a moment on Earth that looked like it was the mid-1700s. We were standing somewhere very agrarian, with rolling green hills all around and the occasional farmhouse with a barn dotting the landscape. I had a knowingness that we were in the eastern United States, somewhere like Indiana or Ohio. I could sense a town nearby, but we had moved to a more isolated property. I heard arguing. A man in period dress came out of the farmhouse. He was purposefully walking toward a huge barn and outbuildings, but he suddenly detoured toward an area that had a shed near a large stack of wood. There was a house nearby, and an axe embedded in an old tree stump near the woodshed.

I could see all manner of cordwood laying around in various stages of being cut, with different sizes stacked together in piles. The farmer was in a rage and was striding right for the axe. He was young, I guessed in his early twenties. I could tell he had been arguing with his young wife. They had been married for 5 years. The Grim Reaper and I were watching a scene play out that had occurred centuries before, however, it didn't diminish the emotions I felt from the farmer nor the rising horror in my mind. I knew what was coming. I wanted to call out. I wanted the man to stop. I so badly wanted to calm him down and make him not do what I could see in his mind he was going to do.

The man grabbed the axe and headed back into the farmhouse. Death reached over and gently hugged me to him. He could feel my sensitive nature rebelling at what I knew was coming. I don't care how many times people have done this or how many years had passed from the event, it still caused me to violently shudder and grieve. I wanted better for both souls involved. I grabbed handfuls of Death's cloak and covered my eyes while plugging my ears with folds of fabric. I didn't want to witness or hear anything of what came next. It was bad enough to feel all the emotions of this moment in my hyperaware state as a soul-traveling mystic. I felt all the rage, the blind emotion that was unthinking and how the man was moving about with a singular thought in his head that repeated over and over. He was going to "do" something about "this."

The man killed his wife with the axe. Death was merciful to him, the wife, and me by changing the speed of time so it happened super quick. I didn't have to hear or see any aspect of it. Thank you, Grim Reaper. I saw the wife's soul leave her body and watched as other souls escorted her to where she needed to be. The farmer was dragging his wife's body out to the woods at the edge of the property. I watched him digging a hole so the body could be hidden. His thoughts and emotions were of nothing but hiding and covering up all that he had done, like a five-year-old boy who was working hard to hide a broken toy.

Death moved the story forward. Images flashed as time moved ahead like the fast-forward feature on videos. I saw the farmer go through various emotional stages of smugness, glee for getting away with the crime, with his lies and cleverness that kept him from punishment, with his ability to fool the townspeople into thinking his wife had left him for another. Then I saw his anger and cleverness give way to grief and despair. And then, several years later, he hung himself.

Death turned to me and said, "Let's go get him. It was an act of passion. It is time for him to come home." I just stood staring at Death's skull-boned face and didn't really have a clue where this soul could be or how to go about finding him. Most of my training til that moment had been on the astral plane and levels of higher frequency. Like an old radio, I had spent most of my shamanistic time on the FM frequency. I didn't travel the AM frequencies. However, Death just kept staring back at me and I asked, "Can you give me a hin …" I didn't get the rest of the word "hint" out of my mouth before I was dropping like a rock. I felt like I was on a water slide and traveling down a tube really fast, the difference being that as I moved down the frequencies, my body was getting heavier, thicker and denser. It was icky. I didn't like the feeling. I was quickly coming into the mindset of "Let's get in, get out and be done with this place ASAP!" It felt like I couldn't breathe because there was such a heavy weight on my chest. It was so stupid, but I had to keep reminding myself that I didn't need to breathe. I had to remember that I wasn't in a physical body. I was moving about the realms as a collection of energetic signatures. The lower down I fell, the denser, more compact and slower moving I became.

Death and I oozed (that's how slow it felt) out of the end of the tube and landed on concrete feet. Imagine you are the consistency of honey on a cold day and you're trying to squeeze the honey out of a plastic bottle's tiny hole at the top. Then imagine when the honey does hit your biscuit; it lands with a solid clunk. I don't know which sensation assaulted my senses first: the moans and sounds of agonizing souls, the blast of heat from raging fires, the reek of sulfur, or the corrosive noxious fumes racing through my sinuses. I had a mantra zinging through my head to help me, "You don't need to breathe, you don't need to breathe, you don't need to breathe."

The furnace-hot air was a wave over my body causing my face and arms to feel like I was baking in an oven. My skin was sending signals to my brain that it was charring to ash as I stood there and that we needed to get out, *now!* I had to continually remind myself that I was not in a body. I didn't have to worry about a body getting damaged. However, there was the pesky little problem that I was unable to move.

My feet told me that they had been cast into concrete blocks and they were on strike. No moving was going to happen. Before I could start to panic about being stuck in the one place I didn't want to *ever* be stuck, I felt Death reach over and slide his hand into mine. I could feel the bones of his skeleton fingers gently wrap around my hand and tenderly move me forward. I was able to take itty, bitty baby steps as I struggled to move the concrete blocks that called themselves my feet.

This was hell.

Wait? What? I quickly looked around and groaned. I had arrived in hell. A place I had spent my life not wanting to be in, but here I was. No welcome sign. No greeting. No recognition of "You are Here!" Just concrete blocks for feet, moving at a speed that made snails look like sprinters. Ugh!

Death had morphed into Grandfather of the West for a quick moment as he spoke to me about our purpose here, who we were looking for and how we were to move about, but then he quickly reverted to his Grim Reaper form as soon as we moved deeper into the regions of hell. As we walked along, he showed me how each one of these layers or 'frequencies' had all been designed by the souls "trapped" in them. They had all put themselves into these spaces because they thought themselves so awful and so beyond the Love of God. I had no idea how I was going to find the farmer in all this mess. It was so difficult to be in this place! And it was made worse by knowing that these souls didn't have to be here; but I had no idea how to share that reality or to get them to discard their belief system that kept them tethered here.

Grandfather of the West let go of my hand and I was beginning to move about quicker in the denser energies. He carefully moved aside the edge of his hood so I could see his skull and his smile. "Are you feeling better?" Talk about questions being relative! I had thousands of smart-ass retorts begging to be the first off my tongue, but decided to answer with a simple, "Yes, Grandfather. Thank you." What I hadn't expected was the bubble of energy that descended over me. I was being buffered from all the sensory impressions that had overwhelmed me when I first arrived on this frequency. I could still hear Death clearly, but I wasn't being exposed to all the sensory inputs that had been causing me to suffer while down in these levels.

Note to Self: when you travel to hell (literally) to retrieve souls, put a bubble of Love around you before you go. "Got it, Grandfather. Thank you." Geeze, in all my shamanistic practices, I hadn't ever expected nor *wanted* a tour. Guess what? Here I was! In hell. With Death. It seemed part of my training was to experience as well as see all the variations on how souls felt they should be treated. It was worse than anything I would ever put a person through. It was crushing to my tender heart to see some of the punishments people felt they deserved. I would have cried tears of despair had it not been for the mission I was on and the Angel I was with.

I was shown the regions of hell (fire-and-brimstone Christian version) that the revivalist preachers of my Midwestern youth taught me. Then there were the regions of constant war and battle that I remembered from the ancient Greek stories. There were also souls just wandering about as if they were on Earth. Their environment was similar to their Earth experience and they moved about aimlessly. I understood that this was the region I had learned about from the voodoo practitioners I had known while in the Bahamas. They and the Catholic priest I knew used to officiate certain island ceremonies together during the spring and fall tides. According to my voodoo teachers, hell was a place of lost souls who wandered aimlessly for all time without purpose. I freely admit that their version of hell scared me more than the fire-and-brimstone version.

We moved into heavier regions of hell. Yes…it got worse. These lower vibrational spaces did not have the light of fires and the red, orange and yellow of flames to offer some contrast to the region. These frequencies looked monochrome, and this region reminded me of the Fields of Asphodel that the Greek stories described. Let me pause us a moment on our tour of hell and give you a bit of background.

I was eleven years old when I decided to read *Bullfinch's Mythology*. Through this one tome, I learned the essence of the Greek legends and made mental pictures of the various gods and goddesses described in this tome. My understanding of the Fields of Asphodel is that it involves a meadow covered by the flower of the same name, but the souls in this region move about without purpose, thought or understanding. This region is without color but doesn't have the heaviness of depression about it. The tone is one of "lost." I began to realize as I gazed over the scene of hundreds of souls wandering aimlessly that this truly was the Hell the Voodoo priestesses used to tell me about. I shivered and wrapped my arms around my astral body. I knew I shouldn't be cold, but this place felt cold.

Death came up beside me, but he had morphed into an Englishman with sandy blond hair and a mustache, wearing a solid white safari shirt and white pants and topping it off with a white pith helmet. I was startled to see him again, and in a place like this. I had seen him long ago, sitting in my mother's hospital room when I was twenty-one. My mother was dying and on oxygen at the time. She kept pointing to an empty chair in the hospital room and said she would be leaving her body as soon as my aunt (her sister) had talked with her one more time.

I looked over to see who the guide was and saw a man wearing a pith helmet, sitting there smiling. As soon as I thought how strange and out of place he looked, he took off his hat and placed it in his lap and ran his hands through his sandy blond hair. His image and attitude were one of quiet joy and confidence.

Now here he was again. I threw myself into his arms and hugged him as hard as I could. (I know, I do that a lot, but I don't restrain myself when I'm happy!) I connected the memories and realized how much Death had been in my life. Memories raced through my brain as they flipped through my inner eye. It seems Death had been present throughout my upbringing and I was learning all the faces he had donned to be around me, guide me and teach me.

As I hugged him, I smelled the Bahamian hibiscus flowers from our back yard in Pink House No. 2. I heard the waves of the ocean on the Caribbean side of the island. I tasted salt on my tongue, and I felt his hands on my back gently rubbing and comforting me. He calmly stated in my mind, "There are over two million 'lost' souls here. They didn't know what would happen to them when they died, so they came here feeling bewildered and confused. Each one of them thinks they've only been here for a few moments since their death. Help me, my darling, by sending them home."

Total shock. I froze in place unable to think, feel or move. I became a block of cement again. After a moment, I had the presence of mind to feel completely unsuited to the task. Yes, I had cleared properties, cars, animals and people of unwanted energies, but this was like clearing a stadium of over one hundred thousand people. The sheer mass of the project weighed me down and I was already so dense I was going to be eating salad for years just to lighten my body! I almost dropped to my knees thinking of the volume of energy needed to get these souls where they needed to go. When I thought of where the souls were vibrationally, compared to the region they needed to go to (the healing hospital with the blankets in the astral plane), I almost fell to my knees a second time in total despair about the request.

Every soul needed to be cocooned in love and healing so that they could move on to the other vibratory levels that would allow them the space and energy to grow, expand and continue learning. This place didn't serve any of those soul needs. It truly was a holding tank, and not a very pleasant one at that. As I pulled away from Death's hug, I surveyed the huge expanse again. Death suggested, "You know, you don't have to do this alone. There are many who wish to help."

I started laughing, which startled many of the souls close to us. I was laughing because I felt stupid. Here I was thinking I had to do this alone. I had become used to working alone on clearings as a human, but here, in this place. This was something very different. What had made me laugh was a mental image I had been given when I was thirty years old by a friendly psychic who told me, "Never be afraid to ask for help, Janine. The angels sit around filing their fingernails waiting for people to ask. If you don't ask, they can't go against Free Will. This is Cosmic Law!"

When Death had suggested I call in help, I had seen a mental image flash in my mind of a white room with angels by the thousands sitting upon row after row after row of desks like they were in a school room, each one filing their fingernails waiting for "class" to be over so they could go play. All angels love working for Daddy (God) and us. But if we don't ask, they can't go against Free Will.

I turned to Death. He had morphed back into his Grim Reaper image, complete with the staff and hourglass hanging by the silver thread. I mentally called out to the angels and asked any who wished to come to help clear this region of hell, to please do so now. Then as an afterthought, I called in angels of all the religions. I knew that these millions of souls came from myriad cultures. I didn't want my ignorance of their belief structures to limit the way the guides used to escort them to the astral plane appeared. I wanted each soul to be comfortable with who they saw. I watched as various angels walked up to each soul after having morphed into a loved one, a saint or a prophet depending upon that soul's particular need.

Watching that filled my heart with such joy I started glowing. Whatever was used to cloak me in this realm was burned off and I glowed like a sun and the Field began to have color. The monochrome tones were fading out and color was flooding over the meadow. It was beautiful. I closed my eyes and headed for the region these souls needed to be. I could feel my soul getting lighter and lighter as the millions of us moved to regions of frequency that released the heaviness of matter and dark thoughts.

When I opened my eyes, I was sitting in my meditation chair. It was 4 a.m. I had meditated through the night. I climbed into bed knowing I was only going to get two hours of sleep that night and mentally was praying to all the angels, saints and Daddy (God) to give me the energy to be a mommy all day despite the night's work.

I heard a very soft, comforting, whispered reply to this inner prayer as I pulled back the covers and climbed into bed. A gentle male voice responded, "Of course, my darling." And all went black.

Chapter 6:
God Says, "Hi!"

◆

The next morning, I awoke at 6 a.m. and tried to reach my nightstand and turn off my alarm. My arm wouldn't move. I felt like I was made of brick. Slowly my mind began to understand that I was awake, but not fully in my body. Sluggishly, I took a few moments to do some breathing exercises and mentally focused my breath into each body part.

When I was able to move, I lay in bed for a bit and thanked Daddy (God) in my head for helping me walk these many worlds and still function as a mother, teacher and wife. Then a feeling of separation came over me that was excruciating, like a knife in my heart. I had experienced so much over the past two days. After decades of praying, meditating and questioning my existence, my many queries of the Creator had been answered. As I thought over the experiences, wave upon wave of gratitude flooded my being. I started crying. There was no way for me to express through physical form the love I had for Daddy and all of His work.

I curled up into a ball on the bed and cried out of joy, love, and yet, sorrow too. Sorrow that I was so small of a human and my human heart could only love Daddy so little. I felt I loved Him more than my heart could hold. I wanted the ultimate experience of Daddy. I wanted what I had always wanted: to know God as the saints and yogis knew Him. I quickly wiped my eyes as a plan settled into my brain. I had clarity and I knew what I was going to do. I knew that it truly was do-or-die time with Daddy. He was going to talk to me or else!

As soon as I finished up my daily activities of being mother, wife and teacher, I raced upstairs to my meditation room to see what was going to happen in this night's meditation. Three days of amazing meditative experiences had primed me for tonight and I was eager to see what was going to happen. I barely had time to sit in my chair and finish my opening prayer before I was whisked away to the astral plane. As my eyes cleared and I oriented myself, I heard the horns and welcoming shouts before I saw the people making the noise.

It was a party. There was a long banquet table loaded with food and sitting around it was every single saint, sage and enlightened person I had ever studied or read about, along with hundreds of others I had yet to remember. Christ walked up to me first and welcomed me to my Coming Home party. He told me this was being done in my honor and everyone was so happy that I had attained enlightenment. That this was the astral plane's reaction to any soul who achieves the spiritual goal that I had set for myself. Everyone was there. My Guru Yogananda, another Hindu guru called Sai Maa, Mother Theresa, Saint Bernard, Saint Ann and Saint Francis. Sai Maa waved at me from the table as she forked some delicious smelling food into her mouth. There was laughter everywhere. The sound of high-toned bells came to me each time a person reached for a glass. It was all so lovely. I was home. All of these people were my family and they were so happy to see me again, and I, them. As I stood in awe of the activity around me, I wanted everyone to experience this joy, this spiritual celebration, this feeling of community.

As my gaze took in the many spiritual masters and their joy of being together, my mind remembered the trap of "form." Many times, I had read the stories of these same spiritual teachers who encouraged their students to find the formless Source. All of them spoke of the need to dissolve the form we saw. That to truly connect with Source required the seeker to even dissolve the beautiful form of God that was created in their minds. As I looked around this gorgeous venue, I knew I hadn't achieved the supreme goal of my spiritual walk. I wanted a two-way conversation with God. I wanted to know beyond any doubt that I had actually communicated with the Divine. Call me stubborn. Call me ungrateful. Call me a spoiled little princess. That was my goal from the beginning, and I knew I wasn't there… yet.

As soon as I had that thought, Yogananda and Sai Maa rose from the table and walked over to me. Christ was standing next to me. The four of us clasped hands and I felt their thoughts and mine become so connected that my self-identity almost disappeared. As we merged thoughts, our forms became fuzzy and indistinct. It was nothing like I had ever experienced before. My thoughts were vibrating, shaking off limiting beliefs and concepts. Yogananda, Christ and Sai Maa completely integrated into my field and as I looked about myself, I realized I was nothing but Light. I no longer had hands or any form at all. I was pure thought, pure Light. I moved in a direction that felt "upward." As I ascended, the strangest things started to "leave" my consciousness.

The first thing that happened was my concept of language disappeared. Language requires labels and definitions that are limiting and I no longer had words for anything that I was experiencing. I then moved into pure emotion. I felt another shaking go through me and realized all of time and space was being released. The mental image I got was that I was leaving Earth's universe, and leaving spacetime, to move into "other."

I was floating in a sea of emotions all around me now. As I bumped into different emotions, certain thoughts would be triggered. I would bump into grief and I would remember Death, but as quickly as I would think of it, the vision, thought and memory would immediately leave me. It was part of a universe I no longer had a connection to. I was hovering in the space between universes. The emotions that swirled around me were becoming less and less intense. I understood that I was leaving the "world" of emotions as well. I had left the world of 3-D concepts and was now releasing the world of emotions. I felt safe and I felt calm, but even the emotion that I had always called "love" was changing, and I was leaving that small, little word behind as well. I felt the shaking again, as if I was being dusted off.

After being cleared of spacetime and emotions, the next experience that occurred is difficult to describe. How do you convey All-That-Is to others when embodied humans view life from a 3-D perspective? All that I experienced and now relate to you is beyond emotion and doesn't have labels.

To move your consciousness to a state where God resides takes meditation and a discipline to release all need to be in control of *anything*. You have to release control of your thoughts. Release control of your identity. Be vulnerable. Allow everything. The amount of trust and faith a soul must exercise is astounding, but a monumental prize awaits at the end of this road. You remember *all* that you are. You Know who you are, and no one can take that from you. And, bonus, all the questions you ever had about yourself, about this world and why it is set up the way it is, will be answered. To a scholar and mystic like myself, that is the holy grail.

The shaking stopped and I felt myself lose all concept of my mind. I was gently released from all thoughts of myself. Everything I had ever learned regarding what it was to be a child, a wife, a mother, a scientist, a human, an earthling, a resident of the Milky Way, all labels about myself dropped away from my existence.

I was in the presence of the Divine. I was One with the Divine. And all I could exhibit was total, unconditional love, joy and happiness. The Joy/Love was so complete and total that I had no other desire or thought than the Divine One. I rested in that existence. So many times, I had heard Yogananda say, "When the I shall die, I will know who am I."

That was just one of the many, previously confusing, circular sentences that saints had used over the centuries. Others included: "I know, that I know, that I know," and "God and I are One." My least favorite saying, because I understood it the least was: "God is."

Well, I was in that experience now. I understood exactly what these gurus, saints and mystics had noted for centuries. I got it. I was there. Or I should say, I am here. All my questions that I have ever asked throughout my entire life were answered in an instant. God had drawn me into His Bosom, and I was One with Him and all of Creation. I use the term like "Him," but really, there is no gender. It's a habit; I've prayed to Daddy. I've prayed to Momma. There is no difference.

I experienced total bliss while hanging out with the Creator, or while I merged with Source is probably a better way to say it. I merged into All-That-Is without a single emotion or thought to cloud my way. I was my True Self. Then it became time to move back into the illusion of life. I was stunned to realize that the life I lived on Earth was not true. It was a game. It was an adventure my soul had picked to participate in with other souls; a larger adventure of moving humanity up the tonal scale of the Universe to the next rung of expression. Humanity was expanding its consciousness of itself and I was one of hundreds of thousands of souls that had accepted the invitation by Source to be put into bodies to help with the process.

As my soul moved down the frequencies to the Causal Plane where souls choose what sorts of thoughts they wish to have and experiences-in-thinking they wish to explore, I felt a separation tug at me. I realized that I had just entered the first stage of leaving total connection with Source. When that occurred, I saw I was surrounded by nothing but what I call the White Space (the same space that my earlier guide to heaven had shown me). It is a "place" where I go to meet Source. I understood that this was the first stage of incarnation and that I was experiencing consciously the creation of my uniqueness. When a soul asks this question, "What would it be like if I wasn't One?" the soul experiences a small tug. The soul is still highly connected to Source/Divine communication, and there will only be the slightest discomfort from being on this plane of existence rather than communicating as One. As I moved about communicating with other souls on this particular frequency, I saw how we souls create with One to make the experiences needed for the One to better known Itself. And now, here I am going all-circular on you as I try to explain what happened!

The next stage was moving back into the frequencies of having emotions and identifying myself with a certain life. When I felt more and more self-identity coming into my field, I clung to the energy and knowingness of One. I moved down the frequencies to slower and slower moving vibrations, and was assured, over and over, that I would never again lose the knowledge, emotion or understanding of what I had experienced. I would not have to go through the mental loss or emotional loss of being separated from One again. My Creator, my Source was with me the entire way back into the body.

As is typical of my experiences, while I was returning to this life, We/One/Source, made a few detours along the way so that I could better understand my purpose on Earth. I would be given a new spiritual dispensation or spiritual "job" to do upon my return. As I left All-That-Is and moved into the 3-D space of this universe again, Daddy initially remained within me as a brilliant orb of light in my heart as well as a field of Love all around me.

However, he switched me into a form again so that I would be more comfortable in the three dimensions of spacetime. He knew how challenged I would be on my way back into the body and was easing me into the noise and turbulence of this vibrational frequency. It is a bit of a bumpy ride coming down the cosmic shoot of manifestation, and I had lots of beings assisting me with buffering as I re-entered the sensory barrage of individuality. As we moved into this Earth's dimensional space, I was given a quick tour of just how big our universe is, and I was shown the layers upon layers of energy and dimensions that make up this one Universe. We moved through the stars so I would get a perspective on the distances and time. We were moving faster than light and I remember having a quick thought of, "But Stephen Hawking wrote that nothing could move faster than the speed of light." Daddy laughed and mentally said to me, "That's because he doesn't know how to bend the rules of Cosmic Law."

I recognized the Milky Way and we moved toward it. I was looking for certain star patterns and realized we were on the wrong arm of the Milky Way. As soon as I thought that, I realized my identity as a "human" and more specifically, an "earthling," had returned to my consciousness.

I asked Daddy why we were on this side of the Milky Way, and I was shown different forms of microscopic life and planets that were in the process of having life created in certain star systems within our galaxy. It was beautiful to see. My heart went out to all the different forms of life that were growing. Daddy was sharing all of this with me like a proud parent. He is proud of how much we humans have learned over the last seven hundred years about ourselves. He is proud of our having managed to leave Earth and send out telescopes to expand our understanding. He said all this like any parent brags about their baby's first tooth, walking, finishing kindergarten, graduating school, getting married and finishing a goal. It is fun to see Daddy so proud and so happy for all humans.

Finally, our return journey slowed, and we were hovering over Earth. We were on the night side of the planet. Daddy spoke rather quietly to me, "Change it. Change anything you want. I will change any aspect of this planet and its creation right now. Tell me and it is yours." My mind raced over all the things I could have changed, world hunger, poverty, disease, war and disasters. As my mind flitted around looking at all the things I have always wanted to change about Life, I reached out to the seven billion-plus people that were down on the planet below. I reached out with my mind and asked all of us at once, "What did we want?" The amount of feedback I got was deafening, but I waited until I heard every single prayer, request, demand, ultimatum, ceremonial song and rite. For a brief moment, I knew everything going on in everyone's mind. I was shown in that moment how little of what we think about the universe truly comes from us, and how much of what we think is instead conditioning from being on this planet. I was shown what good and evil really is and why people are the way they are. I was shown thousands of different perspectives on the same problem and the hundreds of solutions that people had decided were "the" solution. All of these perspectives were "right."

I turned to Daddy and said, "Everyone is getting exactly what they want. I can't have you change anything, Daddy, because our world is operating perfectly. It is functioning exactly the way everyone is thinking it."

Daddy was next to me as a white shimmering cloud of light. I could feel Him smile and He hugged me. "Exactly. Now go help My Children learn what you know."

"What? Wait a minute! How am I supposed to do that?" I asked.

"Do you know what they think down there?" Of course, He did. I was being rhetorical with God here!

"They are still arguing over which version of you is the correct One!"

I gave these and many other protests (Including cussing. I have kept this text PG rather than the R-rating Daddy heard, as He understands cussing can be a way of expressing true emotions for me.) I went on like that for a long bit, listing off every reason I could think of for why this wasn't going to work. I ticked off all the reasons on my metaphysical fingers: People who say they talk to God are considered crazy. People are still arguing over "right" and "wrong." People don't remember their connection to everything. Then Daddy said the one thing that I couldn't resist. No amount of logic, debate or reasoning could fight His request. He simply said, "Would you do it for me? Teach what you know of Me to My Children."

My mind wanted to scream, "EMOTIONAL BLACKMAIL!"

"No Fair!"

"That's *$#@ 100 percent *not fair!*"

He knows me too well. Sigh. My heart instantly melted. I felt Daddy's total Unconditional Love hovering in front of me as we floated thirty-five miles from Earth's surface. He had just shown me so many levels to His domain and had integrated a piece of His thought processes with mine so that I could share that understanding with people on the planet. He had revealed as much to me as He could so that I would have clarity of purpose and a foundation for the rest of my life on Earth. Every question I had ever had about Life, the Universe and Everything had been answered. As a scholar, this is a form of love that goes beyond language. I turned to Daddy and said, "I will do my best, but I will need help."

Daddy laughed at that, "Of course." In that instant I was shown all the help that surrounds our planet as well as the numerous forms the help takes. I was shown all the souls that had reincarnated with me to be my friends, clients, fellow healers, teachers and students, as well as the mystics destined to help me with this particular mission. I knew I had my work cut out for me because of all the things I saw in that moment. There was so much!

Daddy moved us closer to Earth and I could see it was time for daybreak where I lived. As we moved over North America, my eyes tracked to where I lived. My life and all its memories came flooding back; my connections of spirituality, nationality, career, family, marriage all came over me and I felt heavier. My soul was taking on the disparate forms and cultures that I had been exposed to. I remembered I had been married for over twenty-two years and had four children. Ah, there it was; the labels of individuals. I remembered we all had names here; Janine, Brad, Sean, Beth, James, Clare, Bonnie. Then came the labels of relationships to each other; Mom, Dad, Son, Daughter, Sister, Aunt, and so on. As all the names, relationships and people I knew came flooding back into my consciousness, I saw webs and strings of light zipping through the air, connecting me with all of them in an instant.

I realized that I had basically died, and I was coming back to Earth with a totally different worldview. I was changed. I remembered who I really was. I no longer had amnesia. The challenge was now getting back into my heavy body of cells and tissue while trying to explain what I Knew. I hugged Daddy one more time and He directed me to the White Space, the region of formlessness that I carried around within me. It would be the section of "me" that was always connected to Daddy. I turned and began my journey into the physical plane we call home. I took on all the labels, emotions, thoughts and experiences of my present life. I opened my eyes and I was home sitting in my meditation chair.

"How was I to teach what I had just experienced?" my mind asked me.

"Work on that later, Janine. Right now, focus on breathing," was the suggestion Daddy gave me.

"Oh, right! We haven't done that yet, have we?"

I took a breath. It felt weird, alien. I felt like I was breathing for the first time. I had to bring tension back into my body in order to get the muscles to move. I felt every muscle. I could see through my skin, see into my body, see how the assorted muscles and tendons worked as I wiggled the fingers of my left hand. My left side seemed to respond to my mental signals before the right side came "online."

I exhaled and then took in another big breath. I slowly pulled air in through my nose in a long, slow fifteen-second breath and then breathed it out in quick bursts going "huh-huh" out of my mouth. I did this two more times and felt like I was "back." I went to stand up and I felt two hands push down on my shoulders and Christ's voice popped into my head.

"Whoa, there. You're not quite ready for that yet. Take a few more moments. Direct the energy in your heart to all the extremities and make sure to bring a helmet of energy from your heart to cover your head." And then Christ said, "You may want to wear a hat for the next few days. Your head is going to be quite tender. You're still open to the Cosmic Energy being downloaded into your crown chakra right now."

I felt mute at this moment. I wasn't thinking and had lost language momentarily. I felt odd, like my processors were all running, but I was definitely in a reboot phase of my actual brain. I wiggled my toes and my fingers, sending electrical pulses through my body from my brain. Sensing that I had stabilized, I went to stand up again. This time I made sure to move slowly and to act like I was getting out of bed after having the flu. That seemed to work. I heard the word "re-covery" in my head and I knew that I was recovering from an extra-ordinary experience (duh!) and needed to move like a sloth rather than my normal hummingbird, mom pace.

I made it up onto my feet and walked a few steps. I grabbed the doorframe as I got to the door of my room and realized how everything looked different to my eyes. I could see the actual items in the physical world, but I could also feel them without touching them. It was the weirdest thing. I was feeling and seeing at the same time. This was different from the empathic abilities I had always used. This "feeling" was more like I could sense Daddy's consciousness and energy vibrating through everything.

Recognition clicked in my brain. Ah, this is what a few of the saints had meant when they wrote, 'If God were to forget us, His Creation, for one instant, all that we see would be gone in a blink of His eye. We would cease to exist.'

I understood that now. They were right. I could see and feel the consciousness of God in everything. I felt the Masculine projection of Daddy and the Nurturing Creation of Mommy. Both were equally present and created this 3-D reality. How was I supposed to explain this to people? I pushed that thought away. Right now, I needed to get some breakfast made for my family. I hadn't slept much in days, but I didn't seem to need sleep. I didn't need food. However, I did need to move.

The more I moved about, the better I became at navigating around in the body. I felt the thought of, "wiggle your fingers," but when they wiggled, it felt like the message had a long delay and someone else with a joystick had just moved them. Daddy really had rewired me and rebooted my software. And I felt like I had been given some massive upgrades to my programming and needed time to integrate all of the new information into my thought processors.

Walking gently down the hallway, I dragged my hands down both sides of the walls and moved to the staircase. I could feel the entire house with the electricity pulsing through the walls like blood running throughout my body. I could feel every member of my family in their beds sleeping. I knew their breathing rates, heart rates and what stage of sleep they were in. I could tell that my youngest was only fifteen minutes from waking up and was starting to roll around as her breathing began quickening. She was pulling out of deep sleep. I needed to get breakfast made. I decided on oatmeal for its simplicity.

As I continued my slow journey to the stairs, I carefully concentrated on making sure each foot landed on the floor before making the next step. It seemed that spacetime was still shifting in my brain because the floor appeared to be undulating before me. I stopped halfway down the flight of stairs and looked out the front-door windows. Sunlight was streaming through the glass and I was stopped short. There were breathtaking rainbows on the wood floor, and I could see the dust motes dancing in the air currents of the house. I was transfixed.

As I looked at the dancing motes, they moved and shifted in a rhythmic pattern and suddenly they became stars and constellations of a Universe that Daddy had shown me the previous night. I was viewing both experiences at once. Daddy said to me, "You are in both places at once. Your consciousness resides in all places at once. You choose to focus on this life and now." The stars left my vision and the sun's light had shifted position on the floor.

I had a feeling I had been standing on the same spot longer than for a quick communication because Clare came up behind me and asked, "Mom, what's for breakfast?" I immediately hugged her, wished her good morning and focused on tending to the needs of the youngster in front of me. Universes, parallel timelines, multiple dimensions, spacetime and ancient mystical knowledge would have to wait. There were people to feed, dishes to be done, laundry to be washed and a New Year's season to celebrate.

Chapter 7:

The Devil Introduces Himself

◆

In order to truly appreciate the duality, we souls create here on Earth it is important to understand the purpose of the dark side. Back in my childhood, an unexpected visitor laid the foundation for my commitment to a spiritual life through sheer terror. I've shared with you the beauty and joy of finding God, but what drove me to this journey started while living in the Caribbean.

Being raised in a military family, I lived with the constant reminder that my parent's occupation was life-threatening. I was lucky. In my case, my dad had survived multiple naval tours in Cambodia, Korea and Vietnam. He has seven scars on his body from the number of times a bullet had hit him without killing him. My parent made it back from war. Much of our tours of duty after the Nixon era were peaceful, but Death was a constant companion in my life. If it wasn't my dad's occupation that might kill him, there was my mom's long, slow fight with terminal cancer. Death was as much a member of my family as a pet dog or cat.

When I was ten and living on the island of Eleuthera in the Bahamas, I had an experience that would alter my worldview significantly. We were in Pink House No. 2 (there were two houses on my street; guess the color of Pink House No. 1?) and I had been playing all evening in the yard. I was inordinately tired and was struggling to find a way to keep my eyes open. Dinner had been light, and I just wanted to go to bed. I was having trouble breathing, but it was more of a discomfort rather than a full-on asthma attack. I was labeled as having asthma, but I now know it was because both of my parents smoked, and I was allergic to cigarette smoke.

As I got into bed my breathing became more labored. I had learned a trick when I was younger on how to talk to my lungs. It wasn't something I shared with anyone, but I had learned that if I took a moment and calmed my fight-or-flight response, I would feel the muscles around my throat and chest unclench. The feeling of a boa constrictor squeezing the breath out of me would leave and I would relax and fall asleep.

This night was different. I was having difficulty getting a breath. I was able to breathe in a shallow way, but the deeper breaths were impossible. As I continued to work the techniques of breathing that I had developed for this sort of emergency, the constriction got tighter. I had a band around my chest that was getting thicker and tighter. I felt like a giant had taken my torso and was grasping me so tightly that the breath couldn't make it past the upper quarter of my lungs, I was fighting for my life and I knew that if I didn't find a way to relax, I would die.

As I closed my eyes and focused on breathing, I heard my sister call out to my mom because the rasping, crackling sounds of asthmatic breathing were getting louder. I opened my eyes to see my mother looking at me with her stern expression she usually reserved for people who were asking her a medical question. I was unable to breathe enough to speak to her, so I just kept focusing on my breath.

She bundled me up in my blanket and stuffed me into the car and proceeded to drive eighty miles an hour down island roads to get me to the corpsman. The military didn't have a doctor stationed on the base, we had a medic with lots of training. My mother got me to the corpsman in time to receive medical treatment that allowed my breathing to expand. I got a reprieve. As I became drowsy from the medicine as well as the relief of being able to breathe, my mom drove me home so I could rest in my own bed.

The spiritual vision I received upon this night's sleep would define the rest of my mystical life. My response to this vision would bring about my single pointed determination to always look for the positive in any situation no matter what occurred. This experience would result in my personality being labeled as "idealistic" for the rest of my life.

The dream I had that night was terrifying. I lay in my bed enjoying the sensation of being able to take in deep, long breaths of air and letting them out slowly and then breathing in deeply again until I couldn't take any more air in and then letting it out again. I was relishing my breath in a way that only asthma sufferers do. I realized that I would never want to drown after having been through a similar process that night. I made a mental note to make sure I became a strong swimmer and drifted off into twilight sleep. I felt the warmth of my body heat from my covers and mattress while my mind experienced the bobbing sensation of being in a small boat drifting aimlessly on the sea. I don't know how long I was asleep, but I awoke into a dream already in progress.

The heat was the first thing I experienced. Blazing heat was searing my face and the backs of my hands. As I came to consciousness, I realized I was standing in a ring of fire. As I stood there in my nightgown surrounded by twelve-foot tall flames, I had no emotion. It was more like I was just taking in my surroundings and I was trying to figure out what to do next. I turned in a circle to find that there wasn't a break in the fire anywhere, and then my attention was drawn directly in front of me.

There, a small parting of the flames could be seen and the heat on my face lessened a bit. I felt the break in the wall of flames first. Something was starting to pass through the flames. It was a startling reaction for me to feel a thing first before seeing the being. This creature was dressed as a man. My first reaction to seeing this "man" was abject terror. I had heard the word "terror" before in my reading and hearing people talk about being scared, but this feeling went way beyond scared for my ten-year-old brain. This sort of feeling caused the fight-or-flight response to kick in so hard that I literally thought my heart was going to leap out of my chest and fall to the floor throbbing. In the dream my heart was hurting, and I could hear the torrent of pulsing blood rushing into my brain. My head ached with a pressure that was trying to push my skull open from the inside out. As I watched, the hands of this being parted the flames, like drawing back a stage curtain, he came through the ring of fire and stood before me grinning.

My body was involuntarily shaking from fear. This creature looked like a man, but my mind was screaming at me that he was no man. He was unnaturally skinny, and his pale skin had never seen the sun. His hand pulling back the flames was the first thing I saw, so my young mind, naturally, focused on his hands. The skin stretched over the bones so tightly that you could see the veins like mountains that shaped the back of his hands.

As my eyes moved up from there to his spindly arms bearing a black jacket, I took in his thin torso, tiny neck and revolting expression below a black stovepipe hat. His large brimmed hat had a large buckle on the front. His shoes were black with similar buckles to his hat. He was dressed like the pictures they had in school of the early pilgrims that settled the United States.

He wore a shortened cape that moved about in the waves of heat. I would learn later that what he was dressed in was a shaker coat that has multiple layers of fabric over the shoulders that are cape-like. He moved with a certainty of purpose that would allow no compromise. He *was* the last stop. If you came before him, there was no other recourse for you. His word was law. And in his certainty, he would allow no other opinion, perspective, or individuality to exist. He was the closest thing my young mind could process as pure evil. His smile was one of malice, hate and cruelty. He relished in others' despair. He enjoyed delivering pain.

The deeper the darkness in your soul, the better he liked it, manipulated it and created deeper darkness for you to fall into. As he smiled at me, grinning with a knowledge of the intimate places of my fear, he lifted his hand as if beckoning me. I screamed in my dream and my brain burst into fireworks. I was enveloped in flames, burning alive as fire entered my mouth and dove into my throat.

I awoke to my mother leaning over me and unbuttoning my collar. My seven-year old sister was across the room whimpering in her bed. She was scared and sitting up curled in a ball with her blankets and Winnie the Pooh bear. My mother was feeling my head and trying to help me breathe by propping me up on more pillows and asking me why I was screaming. I realized I had broken out in a sweat that had soaked my sheets and nightgown. I was shivering like I was chilled, but in the warm tropics this usually meant that you had a fever or had experienced a shock.

My mother was asking me questions. Could I breathe? Why did I scream? And such. I was still trying to process this dream that had been unlike any others as a child. My thoughts were trying to put together what this pilgrim-like man was and what the ring of fire and other such events had meant. My shivering was the remains of the fear I was still experiencing and the shock, rather than the result of being ill or cold.

I had never experienced such hate before, never felt such malice and disgust emanating from another being. I came to understand over the course of my life that what I had experienced was the "devil," or as close to his energetic signature as my ten-year-old mind and heart could interpret. It would define for me what "bad" really was. I also knew that my behavior would have to be exemplary throughout my young life if I was going to stay alive for any length of time. I felt marked, watched and monitored by this thing.

This Black-Cloaked Man would be my definition of "The Devil" throughout my life. He was true Evil. He would be my personal boogie-man and the reason other kids labeled me "Goody Two-Shoes" and "stick-in-the-mud." No matter what I did on this planet, I knew that Black-Cloaked Man was watching me and waiting for me to slip up in some way. I wanted to avoid at all cost any experience that lowered my energetic signature, as that would bring me closer to him. It would take me thirty years to meet him again and, when I did, he would show me the true meaning of Evil.

Chapter 8:

Dealing with Demons

◆

Fast-forward thirty some years and I'm living in Colorado with my husband, Brad, and our four children. Before I can share the full extent of the Devil, True Evil and the Devil's BFF, I need to describe how I got involved with dark energies to begin with.

The house that we had recently purchased in Boulder County in 2007 had three stories. There was the nicely lit, finished basement where Brad and I had offices, which suited us perfectly. I could shut the door to this level for quiet while counseling my clients who sought financial advice and while recording sessions for my radio show. Brad could work any time, day or night, while home without being disturbed by the family's constant comings and goings. The first floor had the living room, dining room, kitchen and a den, and the top floor, the bedrooms and laundry room.

A part of the basement felt weird. The kids and I noticed it when we first moved in and Brad said he could sense something off about it when he worked late at night. The entire basement had been carpeted but that part, where a small square section of flooring had been covered in vinyl. It was an odd place to have vinyl, but the flooring looked good and Brad liked the fact that he didn't need a mat for his desk's rolling chair, so we didn't think much about it as we grew accustomed to our neighbors and living in Colorado. As we settled into our routines, it became apparent that the house we were in was a well-built home, but that there was something wrong metaphysically.

One night while I was meditating, I suddenly felt the need to protect myself. In the twenty-plus years that I had been meditating, this had never been needed and tweaked my brain. Why? Because I had come to trust that as long as I was meditating and focusing on God, nothing, and I do mean, *nothing*, could touch me in that state. Meditating on God forms a sacred contract between you and the Divine. Nothing is allowed to disturb that bond between God and His child reaching back out to Him.

For the first time in my decades-long spiritual journey, I was feeling threatened in my sacred space. It was so novel that it shocked me. I had had experiences before where I felt someone behind me while I meditated. As unnerving as that was, I later came to understand that feeling. When I would go to a certain level in my meditation, I would start to feel beings around me that were the protectors, guides and spirits that were helping me get back to remembering who I was and how God worked in the Universe. These beings were present in my meditation to help me. But this feeling was not that of angels, sages, guides or saints; this was dark. This was not happiness and light, but the opposite.

As I sat in my meditation chair, facing the images of my Guru and the spiritual giants who had walked this sacred path before me, suddenly I felt a bubble of protection pop over me and "they" were next to me. Three demons were around my bubble poking at it and trying to get into it. I was stunned. What was I to do? I had never had evil of this metaphysical kind come into my field while awake. I was in the most sacred and holy of places as far as I was concerned. I had a rock-solid contract in my spiritual understanding that *they* were not allowed into this space. Why were *they* here?

I was in a panic. My heart was hammering, and I was confused and didn't know what to do. Immediately, I called out to Heavenly Father for help. My bubble strengthened and shimmered, but I could still see the demons. Their pointed fingers could manipulate the bubble's surface. It was malleable and I knew there was something else I was supposed to do.

My heart was beating so rapidly that I felt like a rabbit caught in a cage. I was truly in dire straits, my husband was traveling out-of-state; my children were asleep in their beds and I couldn't move. I was frozen in place. No one could help me. What could I do?

I frantically searched my memory for a story to give my brain something to work with. I needed any story of a saint, sage, yogi or prophet in all my study and scholarship who had experienced anything like this. My mind nearly seized up, but one small area was working despite the rising panic and fear. Then, click, a memory popped out of archival storage and, spiritually, I yelled out for Paramahansa Yogananda. He had been attacked by demons; as I'd read about it in *Autobiography of a Yogi*. His experience with demons had been different in that they had jumped on his chest and stopped his heart. At least, my heart was still pumping, but I could see that I was on a timeline. My bubble of protection was there for only a short while and the demons would make it through unless I figured out a different solution to this metaphysical problem. What had Yogananda done in his panic? He had called out for his Guru. I did the same.

Bam! One minute I was fighting for my life, threatened by darkness and demons and just as suddenly, nothing. I was sitting alone in my meditation chair. A feeling of such love, peace and calm descended upon me that I felt the powerful hand of the Divine hold me and lift me up.

I realized that it had been a test. Daddy had allowed the demons into my field to show me a new way of working with His Universe. This was the initiation into a larger understanding of His Creation as part of being primed for The Calling. I had just been tapped, but for what?

The next morning, I made phone calls to figure out what was going on in my house with the demons. I describe in volume one, *Seeking the Divine: An Intimate Journey into the World of Mysticism*, the chain of events that led to clearing our house of a mystical portal that was pouring out dark energies. I also explained how I came to work with different Native American tribes from over sixteen separate nations.

My life would become much different than before the demons. God had work He wanted me to do with a group of people that I knew little about. But I had a more important job to do in this moment. My husband would be returning from his business trip and it was time to explain what had been happening to me spiritually.

Chapter 9:

Enlightenment-A Work in Progress

◆

I had known when I was eighteen and left the Catholic Church that I wanted more from my relationship with God than I could ever achieve using the path that a traditional religion had laid out for me. Here I was, forty-six years old and I had attained enlightenment. I had managed to connect into the thoughts of God and was having two-way conversations with the Divine Lover of All. For many months I stayed quite busy in my meditations as the Divine showed me around the parts of Creation that we forget when we move our consciousness into human bodies. These initial connective experiences were covered in greater detail in my book, *Seeking the Divine: An Intimate Journey into the Realm of Mysticism.*

It took a few weeks, but I was gathering the courage to tell Brad and some of my close spiritual friends what had occurred to me. It's not every day that you have your Hindu Guru and Jesus the Christ appear before you and tell you that you are now an awakened soul and they have work for you to do on the planet. I mean, this is the kind of thing that happens in movies, right? Not to a stay-at-home mother who must worry about dishes, laundry, teaching classes for homeschooling groups and tending to the needs of small children 24/7.

Sure, I had been working toward communicating with God all of my adult life. Now that I had that communication channel open and was receiving nightly advice from Daddy while spending hours touring the realms of Creation, I was struggling to keep my mind grounded on Earth.

At first, I thought I would keep all these experiences hidden in the "vault of my heart," But over time it became apparent that I was meant to let others know. After two weeks of nightly journeys out into the multi-verse of all Creation, I finally decided to tell my husband why I had been sleeping in the basement for the past few days. It was because I hadn't been sleeping. I was having meditations that were lasting all night and there was no difference in my brain from daily life and the nightly journeys I was experiencing with God as my tour guide. I didn't have words for everything that had happened to my brain as God reminded me of all that I am. He was carefully and gently opening recess after recess of my memories and showing me my existence before I became "Janine."

I now knew how Christ was able to stay awake as God showed him Creation.

As I spoke with God about the best way to share with Brad, the man I loved, what was going on with me, I struggled with the desire to keep God all to myself and the need to share His Unconditional Love with others. I was still conflicted, yet in awe. Here I was an accomplished yogi that had managed to have the brass ring of enlightenment handed to her after only twenty-four years of effort. It was something that I had been taught took many, many lifetimes. This was one of many incorrect perspectives I had been told about spirituality, enlightenment and spiritual healing that was going to have to be reorganized in my brain. Much of what I'd learned had become wrong for my life path.

I returned from my tour of "heaven" earlier than normal one morning and went upstairs to make coffee for Brad and me. Our marriage worked well, and we were an efficient and effective team. Over the course of our decades together we had moved seventeen times through nine different states and managed to keep our sanity throughout our nomadic life. We had been married for ten years before we were blessed with children and, as soon as I realized I was going to be a mom, I dropped out of corporate life as an analytical biochemist to raise our family. I didn't think I was going to be able to have children; the fact that we ended up having four was thrilling to me, but a little shocking to Brad.

Brad and I were both scholars and scientists. We were well suited to one another's personalities because we had inexpensive tastes and enjoyed the simple things in life. He and I had met while in college. He was one of the few people I knew who actually had a plan for his life. He also has a delightful sense of humor and looks like a five-foot-ten version of comedian Drew Carey from "Whose Line is it Anyway?"

Brad had come down into the kitchen to prepare for his day, and I asked him if he had any pressing issues or clients to deal with that morning. As a veterinary pathologist, he had managed to work out multiple consulting contracts for several pharmaceutical companies that kept him traveling and working solidly for nine months out of the year. So, he was often gone from home three weeks a month. When home, he spent a great deal of time catching up on paperwork, the kids and I's activities and writing.

Before Brad headed down to his office, I asked him if I could chat with him about something important since he didn't have anything pressing with work. I told him that after decades of seeking God, I was having intimate conversations with the Big Guy nightly as He showed me around the Cosmos.

With a tight throat and a queasy stomach, I did my best to explain the spiritual dispensation I'd been given by Christ and my lineage of Gurus. Yogananda had directed me to go out and help the Native American nations as a Sacred Clown (someone who follows certain customs to heal tribal members). Brad listened quietly while my story spilled out about having Christ's hands on top of my head in diksha, about how Christ had taught me how to heal the people who came to me, about how the heaven I experienced was much different and much more expansive, than the Catholic version I'd been taught or anything my scientific brain could have dreamed up.

As I wound down my experiences and opened my ears to truly receive Brad's reply, he simply asked, "What does that mean for you?"

"I don't know, honey, I'm still figuring that out," was the only answer I knew to give. Brad had always been extremely supportive of my spiritual walk. He was the first to admit that nightly meditations, spiritual retreats and my passion for reading about saints and sages was not his cup of tea, but he always supported my need to pursue a mystical life. He headed downstairs to work since I didn't have any further information to share.

Over the next few days, I told a few close friends about my experience with Christ and Yogananda. Most said they had sensed a difference in me, or that they had suspected for a time that something big was coming into my life. I had one friend give a huge sigh of relief and say, "I've always known you were my teacher. I've just been waiting on you to accept your spiritual role!" He then shared with me his heart's desire for God and asked me my advice on meditation and shamanism.

What I was becoming, in a broader sense, was a mystic who focused on metaphysical healing at the most basic level. No matter what aspect of the Divine a person felt connected to, Mother, Father, Friend, or Beloved, I now knew that my job went beyond helping tribes to helping individuals remember their *own* intimate connection to Source. So, the easy decision for me, despite the isolation it created for a time, was to not affiliate myself fully with any one tribe, religion, or spiritual system.

I decided to continue to align myself only with Source, and to work with people where they were and not to place any expectations about their need to be in or join a particular faith, group or dogma. I wanted the students who wished to learn from me to follow their own inner promptings rather than have another system of faith imposed upon them. My job was to give them metaphysical guideposts along their spiritual journey and provide support and paradigms from different perspectives as their path unfolded before them.

With this decision made, I was rewarded in that night's meditation by Grandfather of the Stars appearance. A quick introduction is needed on this spiritual teacher. Grandfather of the Stars is one of many immortals who guide human evolution on planet Earth. It wasn't until Paramahansa Yogananda's book, *Autobiography of a Yogi*, was published in the 1940s that mystics were able to connect the dots and share that this being was also Mahavatar Babaji. That book is how I came to learn of this Divine teacher.

However, Native Americans in North America have a different name for this being. When I would describe this guide with his long cloak made of the fabric of the Universe, his raven black hair down to his waist and his youthful twenty-five-year-old appearance, I have had Native American shamans state with awe and reverence, "Ah, that is Grandfather of the Stars." And then they would share with me their particular tribe's perspective on this great being. I have since learned the names and images that three major religions use for this being based on spiritual manuscripts and mystic's visions. For my Judaic brothers and sisters, he goes by the name Archangel Metatron; and he has shown up as one of the Immortals in the Mormon tradition based on Josef Smith's writings, and as Babaji by many Hindu traditions.

Because I had decided what type of teacher I wanted to be while living on Earth, Grandfather of the Stars had appeared to me, and we spiritually traveled through time. He showed me lifetime after lifetime where I had been a nun, knight, guru, Celtic clansman, medicine woman, Native American warrior, Buddhist monk, and Egyptian priestess. All of these lives as a spiritual leader or teacher or follower flashed through my mind in seconds and I knew that I had made the correct choice for this life. I had the memory of all those other lifetimes of working with people now available to me as a resource, and it was obvious from the general overview that my current life was best served by my choice. I would be a friend, teacher, minister, guru, healer, guide, shaman, and clown. I decided that no one label would work in this lifetime, except the one coined by the Native Americans in the early 1700s; Sacred Clown.

Quickly my mind made the connection to *The Lord of the Rings* series by J.R.R. Tolkien. The main wizard character in that book was Gandalf the Grey who died fighting an ancient demon and came back into the story as Gandalf the White. His character had been transformed by the experience of fighting the darkness and had come back to Middle Earth a stronger, lighter, younger wizard to help guide the heroes to their particular destinies. It was delightful to make that connection. Gandalf traveled from kingdom to kingdom of Middle Earth and, depending upon which kingdom he was in, he was called by a different name and had a different title.

I thanked Grandfather of the Stars for this connection. It made perfect sense to me. Already I had seen a bit of this in play with my own life as I worked with the different Native American tribes. Each tribe I came into contact with gave me a different name. I had only been working with them for a few years and already had Buffalo Woman, Sweet Spring Water, Laughs-with-Crows, White Crow, and Mother Goose (the last one started off as a joke and stuck!) to add to the mix. It seemed each tribe had a different definition and job description that I needed to fill as Grandfather of the West and Grandfather of the Stars moved me around from place to place. The Gandalf model fit, only I didn't have an awesome wizard staff and I still have hat envy for that rocking portable shade Gandalf wears.

As the months passed, I became more and more comfortable with what I knew my role to be. I could say with confidence, "I know why I am on this planet. I can help you find the same, if you want me to." My entire life, I had only wanted God to talk to me in a way that I could understand, and I never wanted to ever lose that connection again. Now, I found myself wanting to help anyone who wanted the same thing. I wanted as many people as possible to know how much they are loved, cherished and guided in their lives while here on planet Earth.

My spiritual focus had shifted. I was to bring as many people into the presence of the Divine as I could. But unlike what I had seen in many Christian religions where they send out missionaries to collect followers, I took a different path. I knew that God would send me students to guide in their own personal journey back to Source. I continued living my life according to my earthly responsibilities, with the added job of Sacred Clown tacked onto my daily to-do list.

Chapter 10:
The Devil's BFF

◆

There is a space in Creation where duality doesn't exist. Where good/bad, black/white, happy/sad, sickness/health are concepts that just don't register in frequency. There is a place in the Universe that has been made for shamans, psychics and mystics to go where they are totally safe and unable to be molested, distracted or harmed by any being in creation. This place looks different to each mystic and comes with symbols, personages and tools based on that individual's traditions, culture and spiritual perspective.

Mine is White Space. Simply put, I've always felt that God was formless. If He was going to be omnipresent, omnipotent and omniscient, He was going to exist for me as a consciousness without form. After my many experiences with various manifestations of Creation, I realized that my safe place was not a place at all; it was a vibratory field where the only manifestation that could enter was one based solely on pure unconditional love. It took me over a year to define this understanding into language. I had experienced my safe place for years before I was able to put into words what I was experiencing and how it felt to be in that region of existence.

This White Space is where I would go during my nightly meditations to chat with God. It was the only experience that I could have where I was in full alignment and connection with my Source. Daddy was always there and happy to chat with me about anything my heart or mind needed to discuss.

There were many nights where I would go to this sacred space and would see Daddy there and we would commune in total silence, enjoying one another's vibrations. Love would speak Love to Love. Sounds so cryptic as I write this, but that is the best way I can communicate what was going on.

Each night, after my enlightenment in 2010, as I sat down to meditate with the singular purpose of talking to my Divine Beloved, I would take in a few deep breaths and relax my body. Almost immediately, I would be in my White Space. I knew that only Daddy and I could be in this space unless I allowed someone else to show up. A part of me had always wanted a part of Daddy all to myself. That selfish, little kid part of me didn't want to have to share Daddy's attention with anyone or anything. I wanted Daddy to be with me, fully connected and fully engaged. This was the place that Daddy and I created to satisfy my deep, childish desire. It was a region of space that vibrated so intensely, that to go to the next level of frequency would require me to leave my body and allow it to "die" because my soul would release all attachment to this life. I wasn't ready for that, yet. There were still experiences for me to have on Earth and I wanted to finish raising my children.

One night, as I wrapped up another journey of retrieving souls (this time a variegated mass of sailors who all died going down on a ship in the Indian Ocean) my soul went up to the White Space to find Daddy waiting for me. This was odd. Normally there would be a short wait for Daddy to appear.

In addition, He was vibrating in a state of eagerness, obviously preparing to share something new and different to my thought processes. I felt a bit of tension that had never been a part of my experience within the White Space. I came to understand that the tension was created by me when I brought a thought process that was inaccurate to the way Source sees things. I would have to change the way I thought about something to harmonize my understanding and allow myself to view creation as Daddy does.

After a quick communion of silence with Daddy upon my arrival, He telepathically informed me that there was someone he wanted me to meet. This sent a bit of a shock through my system, but rather than it being sharp and course like the emotions we experience on Earth, this was more like the brush of a butterfly's wings across my cheek. It was such a strange and novel experience for me. It took me seconds to accept what was changing in the White Space. That was odd. Normally things happened instantaneously here.

This White Space was actually a bubble and could be expanded or contracted to accommodate my desire for total connection with God. As my gaze focused on the outside regions of this space, a being began to emerge into focus that was so energetically dark, I wondered how this being ever made it into our vibratory realm. Then, this being did something rather comical, just like the old Bugs Bunny cartoons, this being unzipped the form he was wearing like a costume and stepped out of it as the most glorious being of light. He radiated with more intensity than Christ, and *that is* saying something.

As he walked into the White Space, I was totally transfixed by his poise, demeanor and attitude. This wasn't an archangel. This was *the* Archangel. This was Morning Star from the book of Isaiah, The Devil as Christians call him. As the top Archangel came closer to me, Daddy became a full-bodied form in front of me. He and Morning Star embraced in a hug that sent my vision into fragments of light and sparks as if fireworks had erupted. I was blinded by their union and in that instant, popped out of the experience; I opened my eyes to find myself in my meditation chair at home, panting as my heart raced in full flight-or-fight mode.

After taking purposeful breaths to get my heart rate under control, I realized I had been gifted with a story from the metaphysical world. Daddy had upgraded my thinking, again. I sprinted to my computer to see if I was thinking about evil and the devil correctly. I wanted to double check and see if what I had just learned fit with the documents, we humans had on Earth.

I had been shown that the devil's BFF was ... God. Morning Star hadn't been cast into hell, he hadn't resisted God. God had given Morning Star a job and Morning Star had taken the job *willingly*. He was playing a role for God, who revealed to me what the story behind that role was.

I realized that the Black-Cloaked Man who left me breathless in my youth had actually helped me learn to prioritize connecting to Source, long before I had those demons poking at me while meditating in Colorado. The whole point of evil in the world (or darkness if you prefer) was to play the role given to them by each of us. Every person in my life who had, "done me wrong" was teaching me what I really wanted from this life by showing me (in no uncertain terms) what I didn't want to become. Now, could I find any documents on Earth that hinted at the devil and God's close relationship that I had been shown through telepathy?

Chapter 11:
Rethinking Villains & Victims

◆

For most of my life, it now appeared, I had the whole idea of evil wrong. The concepts I'd learned of the devil, darkness and sin were not the way Daddy views them, His children or the way we create our lives at all. Yes, that's right. We have full creative rights when it comes to our lives (more on that in a few chapters). Based on what I'd just learned, I had to alter the thoughts I had on evil and Lucifer.

My early training in the Christian perspective of life meant there were still some thoughts in my subconscious mind concerning evil that Daddy needed me to change. First off, Morning Star did not riot against God. They are best buddies and, when God proposed the creation of Man to Morning Star, Morning Star immediately agreed to participate in the event.

This is how the story was laid down in my head when I saw God and Morning Star merge into an arc of white light. As God was working on His plan to create a region of existence for souls to experience, He knew that duality would need to be created first. He knew that His Children were going to require an element of existence to resist them as a palette of options on which to paint their own creation.

There would need to be a force, something to be in duality with, a contrast for the Children of God to work with to keep them in a state of expression as well as of expansion. God charged his closest and dearest friend, Morning Star, with this occupation. For this was the most delicate of tasks, requiring the contrast and resistance to be strong enough that it would drive God's Children to continually express their creativity without shutting down their ability to expand and rise to their full potential.

This duality, this contrast in our world, is presented with as much multiplicity and diversity as each human creates within their own lives. We have over seven billion people on this planet who are creating their own existence in seven billion different ways, each with a unique perspective and understanding of what makes up this world and how it works. As Daddy's version of this story continued to challenge what I had been taught, I felt years upon years of misunderstandings and ignorance fall away from my conscious and subconscious mind.

After my thoughts had been harmonized to how creation truly works (or as much as I could absorb of this massive, grand design), I understood how Daddy kept the contrast in place, with our assistance as His children.

The next night in meditation Daddy showed me how souls make contracts with one another as we determine what sorts of experiences we wish to have on Earth during our lives. I was able to listen in as various souls decided on their relationships with one another before they incarnated into bodies. Each had different experiences they wished to have, and each soul requested certain behaviors from others to receive these experiences. I witnessed two souls as best friends discuss an event that would occur twenty-four years after they incarnated into human bodies on Earth. I was stunned to hear their conversation.

Soul No. 1: "Last time I was the man so this time I'm going to be the woman."

Soul No. 2: "Okay, I'll be the man."

They both changed their forms to reflect their newly acquired roles.

Woman: "I want to experience independence and freedom this time around. So, we'll marry for a period of time and then we'll need to separate. I enjoy our time together and I'd like to end up as friends in the end like last time."

Man: "We can do that, but I'm not going to let you go easily. I'll test you before you gain your independence. How creative do you want me to be? Because you know that I want you to be the most you can be down there. I'm not gonna go easy on you."

Woman and Man harmoniously agreed on their plans.

The challenging part of writing this exchange is that all of this was done telepathically and there were many emotions and past lives flashing through these souls' thoughts as they made multiple decisions on how they were going to live and what sorts of options they were going to give themselves as they moved through the flow of creation. We souls create predetermined events, but then, there are multiple options that will allow these events to occur depending upon our choices and emotional states. There is structure to our lives with these predetermined events, but the way this structure manifests has multiple options. This is where we humans can get quite creative.

These two souls had been best friends many, many times and continued to reincarnate with one another. They were determined to experience life in as many diverse ways as possible. Some of the experiences I had seen as they planned their future lives together were; brothers-in-arms during a variety of battles, husband-wife, mother-daughter, father-son, sisters, brothers, and finally best friends during World War I in Austria where they found themselves fighting on opposite sides of an international war. They were preparing for a new life this time around, together as husband and wife, with the roles reversed from a previous incarnation.

The lesson I walked away with from this exchange was; *there is no villain in our creation*. There are people who treat us badly or are toxic to be around, but they are not villains. All the folks in our lives who make our path easy or difficult were put into our journey to guide us to grow, to expand, and finally, to help us remember who we want to be. Each person, each soul, and each experience define for us our desire to be more and better.

The next lesson I understood was; *there are no victims*. This one was harder for me to grasp and took repeated sessions with the Divine to comprehend and remove from my psyche. I am such a mother and protector of the innocent that I had to be shown repeatedly how to view the events on Earth with compassion rather than sympathy. It was a process that would take months. I would be run through a host of scenarios by Daddy that demonstrated the difference between sympathy, empathy and compassion. Daddy was working on my experiences and thoughts to show me the value of compassion over the other options (see glossary).

After much practice, I came to understand the differences in terms of how these labels were affecting my behavior and thoughts and how they needed to be altered so I could operate at my personal best. It took a lot to rework my emotional and mental reactions, but when He was successful with me, I understood the power a person can gain over their development when they no longer see themselves as a victim or treat *anyone* in their life as a victim. The same was true for not seeing others as villains.

That was the biggest lesson of all for me. That a huge ripple of Light energy emanates from any person who treats everyone in their lives as the powerful creator that they are. Victory in life is not about villains and victims, winners and losers. It is about remembering who you are as a multi-dimensional being. It is the personal victory of your own mind, your own emotions, your own Spirit. This realization stands as my biggest victory of on this planet. I want those around me to experience their own victories as well.

The most surprising aspect of my understanding was coming face-to-face with true evil and then finding that this being, this force and this consciousness had as much care and concern for us as Source does. This concept took me several months of nightly meditation to integrate as I cleared lifetimes of misplaced ideas about how we create our life experiences.

Evil's only job is giving us a backdrop with which we can see the outline of our Divinity. He is trying to get God's Children to remember their Divine inheritance.

This was a tough lesson for me to learn.

But learn it I did.

Chapter 12:
The Afterlife Journey

G od had shown me heaven and Christ had shown me hell. I know that many people have their opinions and perspectives on what all this means to them. The challenge I have in communicating my perspectives to them is that I don't have beliefs. I don't have opinions.

I have *experiences*. I don't talk about heaven and hell lightly. I know they are collective understandings that have taken millions of people centuries to produce and create. They are a work of art that allows people on Earth to have some comfort for their loved ones when they die. They feel the severing of experience of being with their loved ones when the departed cross over to the "other side."

Many movies, books and websites cover what versions of heaven and hell can look like. What I know and teach is based on my experiences and the experiences of the shamans with whom I have worked. As I lay out my structure of the metaphysical levels of life, please know that my understanding comes from a multitude of sources. I continue to adjust my understanding based on insights learned from mystics who have different paradigms. Shamans, psychics and healers will tell me what they know about their experiences in the vast nonphysical worlds and, as I gather more experiential data, I expand my view and understanding of my own experiences.

Over the past nine years of gathering information from hundreds of Native American Shamans, Chinese Buddhists, Mexican Mystics and Jewish Seers, I have created a vast picture of what goes on with souls after we leave our physical bodies on Earth and continue our life in frequencies in the fourth and fifth dimensional realms. Originally, I was doing this for my own benefit. I wanted to make some sense of the experiences I was having. I never dreamed I'd ever share it. There seemed to be so many authors out there that had become gurus, priests and spiritual leaders. I really didn't see where I could add to the conversation. But some physics students suggested otherwise.

While I was teaching in 2004 at a small four-year college in southern Utah, I was helping a group of nine students prepare for master's level classes. At one point in the semester, they requested that I move beyond classical physics and what we call "reality," and speak on topics that were metaphysical. I agreed, but only if the discussions occurred after regular classes and were totally voluntary. By the end of the semester, I was teaching metaphysical matters to twenty-three students, who encouraged me to write a book on this spiritual stuff.

I have found that three different levels exist to the metaphysical worlds I work in. For the purposes of this book, I'm not going to discuss the scientific or science fiction understanding of the multiple-worlds theory, M-theory, parallel universes, the spacetime fabric or relativity. There are places for all of these understandings in a mystic's paradigm, but for the purposes of discussing where we go when we die, I'm going to focus on the three basic realms that souls can go to when we decide to leave our body.

This metaphysical understanding was first introduced to me by Paramahansa Yogananda in his 1946 book, *Autobiography of a Yogi*. In it, he discusses in fine detail the timelines of planetary evolution, the different ages humankind has gone through, and how we are on the upswing of an evolutionary arc. Yogananda does a much better job describing this calendar of human understanding and evolution than I could do, so I will leave you to the reference in the back of this book for personal study. For now, we will focus on the three large levels of soul's existence.

The human is made up of three different vibrational bodies and one formless body. Each body has its own frequency and can be seen by some mystics with the skill of clairvoyance. I understand that "formless body" is an oxymoron but work with me here for the moment. The human is made up of a physical body, an astral body, a causal body and then a formless body of light. The use of body for the formless light body is to give us a starting point for understanding. The physical body is what most humans identify as "themselves" when they say their name. There is complete identification of the name with the body and very little time or thought is given to the name representing the vastness of the soul.

People who understand that they consist of more than a physical body, may be aware of a second plane of existence, which is called the astral plane. This astral plane is the area that most shamans, psychics, tarot card readers, reiki masters, mediums, and mystics operate in. It is where most "go" for information and to talk to loved ones that have crossed over into the non-physical world. The astral realm is much like the physical world. But it lacks cold, heat, hunger, or thirst because those physical sensations are not necessary in the astral realm.

Moreover, there are fantastical creatures in the astral realm that fit with the pictures and concepts we have of dragons, mermaids, unicorns, fairies, elves, and gnomes. And a soul can create instantaneously in the astral realm. This is why young children get so impatient with the physical realm. They more recently existed in the nonphysical realms and often have a clear memory of being able to create whatever they wanted, so they find the whole concept of time and "waiting" to be alien.

We have the ability to see astral images and concepts on Earth when the veil between the realms becomes thin as a result of extensive meditative practice, or when a soul decides it is time to have a conscious awareness of the higher planes of existence.

The third body, also known as the causal body, is harder to explain because it is made totally out of light and barely has any form to it when you are standing in that vibrational space. This frequency has beings that are moving around you with equally indistinct outer edges of form because "protection from other" isn't needed in the way we use it on Earth. This causal plane is the one where thoughts of individuality first originate, whereas the astral plane is where the thoughts become defined, taking on an image or construct that we will use in the physical world. The thoughts and concepts become a "thing" in the physical world when we think about something long enough.

A lot of condensing of waveforms needs to happen from the origin of Source in order for a soul to manifest as a physical human. The causal plane is the area where the soul makes the decisions necessary to bring about the wanted experiences on the next physical journey. The causal realm gives the soul its individuality from Source, and allows each soul to dictate the experiences, perspectives and knowledge it wishes to collect and learn from to further its own personal evolution.

I find the causal realm the easiest to navigate and learn in because of the nature of its vibration as well as the energy of the beings that were moving about in this wonderful frequency. It was here where beings would come up to me and ask for information and would literally use my experiences like a file in a filing cabinet. They would scan all the information and experiences that I've ever had in my life on Earth in preparation for their own life experience. They would research my knowledge of different countries, my perspectives and understanding of humans, and would use that to help make decisions on what society they would allow themselves to be born into, what parents they would have, and other fundamental factors related to where their soul would end up.

I was not the only soul sharing this sort of deep, intimate, personal information. Thousands were in this realm seeking knowledge to make choices for their soul's evolution. There is no need of any kind of protection; all is open, accessible and welcome. There is no judgment of experiences, filtering of information through the lens of morality, or disagreement of choices made, only the sharing of knowledge.

This frequency went *beyond* what we think of as telepathy. (Yea, I know, that was weird for me to experience, too.) Telepathy is slow relative to this vibrational union. Consider the transmission of information in the causal realm to be like the difference between snail mail and email. It is super quick and faster than thought.

On Earth, everything is about the passing of time. We live completely from an understanding that time moves in a linear way, and we gauge the passage of time on events that occur in our lives and how time passes between events. Communication at the causal level involves no sense of space or time. In this frequency, timelines are discussed, but as you move about this level you are not affected by time.

Communication in this realm also occurs without most emotions. Your thoughts are totally your own until you see another soul who could benefit from your perspective. Then that soul will come over to your field and start sifting through your life experiences until the necessary information is found and, with *profound* gratitude, the soul will leave with a tender *compassion* for all you had been through to bring information to them. Privacy does not exist in this realm. You don't need to protect yourself in this plane of existence in pure Love, so why not share all that you know with the beings that need it most?

The only time I had any discomfort while I was experiencing the causal plane was when a particular soul was a bit too determined to sift through some touchy memories of mine to get at a bit of data that he needed for his life path. He wished to be a male in his next life and wanted the female perspective on what being a male was like on planet Earth. He was a bit too thorough in his digging around for how men had treated me in my life, and he got into two areas that I really didn't want to remember.

As soon as I exhibited the slightest hint of resistance, he immediately stopped and asked, "Are you still in a body on Earth?" He seemed shocked that I was in this realm if so. I said, "Yes, I'm sorry, I'm not used to being like this. I have no memory of being here before my incarnation; I'm still learning how to travel the realms while living on Earth." He quickly apologized for being so "rough" and told me a few items he needed to know for his next life. I made recommendations and we moved apart with total love and respect for one another's roles in the Universe's Grand Design.

When I returned to my body that night after meditation, my heart filled with pain as feelings of loss and grief consumed me. I had experienced a love and communication so intense and beautiful in meditation. I knew I had been seeking this type of love on Earth. Realizing that it was near impossible to experience it here left me sobbing. I understood that the only way to share this experience was to find other mystics who had visited the causal plane. If I could find them (and I did through their writings), then there would be that commonality of similar experience. This is what drives me to write, teach and learn. Causal plane Love is that intense.

Now that we've walked through the various levels of a soul's evolutionary journey, let's discuss what happens when a soul dies on the earthly plane. As a soul prepares to leave a body, it has been my experience that the soul provides the means and the situation for its own death. Just as each baby is born when it means to be born, based on the choices it has made beforehand, so does each soul choose the time of its "death" from the body as it casts aside the physical plane for other adventures.

Each soul has control of both of these dates. Because of the spiritual work I do, I totally see now that there isn't death after all; there is just a change of "phase." Much like the French chemist, Antoine Lavoisier stated in the law of conservation of mass, Matter is neither created or destroyed it just changes phase. The same is true of our souls. A soul is neither created nor destroyed along the path of its evolution.

When a soul decides it is time for it to shake off the body and go back to its Source, the death of the body will be timed perfectly for all the participants on that soul's journey to be available for the lessons and discussions that are needed before the parting of ways.

As a spiritual guide, I've been asked many times to be metaphysically present to help a soul back to their Source. I have promised the departing person or their family that I would be spiritually present to walk beside the soul as it leaves the physical realm for the astral realm. My assurance that I would be present as a guide provided comfort while the loved one was still in the body. However, as soon as the soul was free of a physical body, their "dead" loved ones were there to assist them. Actually, those in the afterlife were present, standing around the bed with me, the entire time while everyone waited for the soul to decide on the correct moment to depart. As soon as the soul could see us standing around their dead body, the soul would go with the already "dead" loved ones into the astral plane.

Allow me to explain the "white light" described by people who have had Near Death Experiences (NDEs). This light is the opening between the physical realm and the astral realm. The white light is the formless space between frequencies and is God's Grace or Source's Unconditional Love. The white light is also a collective energy that represents a promise to a soul that, no matter what happens while on Earth and in an incarnated body, the soul will be guided back to the spiritual realm for its next expansive journey on its spiritual path.

This light is so bright and so beautiful that the soul's heart region lights up like a fire while connecting with it, and all the soul wants to do is enter that light and be filled with it. Why? Because it feels fantastic. Better than anything we have here on Earth, and that really is saying something when you think of all the amazing things here that give us comfort; a child's hug, hot cocoa, fuzzy warm slippers, soft, cushy pajamas, that perfect chair that you lie back in as the footrest lifts you off the floor. Try to imagine anything that brings more pleasure than watching a butterfly dance in a sunbeam, seeing dewdrops of water reflecting the light off a lawn in the early morning, or making love with a partner you fully trust.

This light is the guidance we are guaranteed before we ever enter a body. Some mystics even have a highly structured path they go through to enter the white light. Yogananda used to discuss how, after his enlightenment, he would see a white star surrounded in a field of blue, with a gold ring around the blue field. This was his vision of a path he began to travel each time he meditated. He eventually used this path as part of Self-Realization Fellowship's trademarked symbol. This movement into a white light experience is one I have had over and over again for years since I became enlightened.

This white light or white star is the portal that shamans, psychics, tarot card readers, mediums and mystics use to remove the veils of physicality from our sight and look into the astral plane to gather the information we are asked to retrieve for people back here on Earth.

As a soul leaves and observes the scene around their physical body, life no longer holds sway on their identity of self, even though they observe grieving family and friends. The soul will automatically rise above the situation and will experience the layers upon layers of our 3-D reality from a new, four-dimensional point of view.

That is not to say that entering the astral plane is always simple. If a soul becomes anxious, nervous or uncomfortable at any point, family members, past lovers and friends that have already died will rush in to provide comfort as the soul continues to rise above the planet and enters the portal that brings it to a familiar, comfortable space. Then, the soul is welcomed home as the long vacation on Earth ends.

It is a sweet reunion of friends during which, at any time, the soul may turn and see their body lying in repose as family and friends on Earth grieve over the perceived loss. The soul, meanwhile, feels tremendous joy and a big sense of relief for entering a space of infinite freedom. Many souls will take huge, deep breaths because of the habit from breathing on Earth. The soul is remembering all that was forgotten when they had made the choice to live as a human.

As the soul moves further into the astral plane and is welcomed by more and more friends and family, a guide appears that is a long-time friend of the soul. This has been the agreed-upon guide for the soul's journey to the next phase of remembering. Depending upon how the soul died, their earthly experiences and the desire of the soul in that moment, the soul will be taken to healing spaces with gardens, cabins, gazebos, brightly lit buildings or running waters and hot springs. Based on the soul's last incarnation experiences, these healing spaces will be perfectly customized to fulfill the soul's understanding of perfection, rejuvenation, refreshment and renewal.

At times a family has asked me to go find a soul after its death. I've often traveled to a healing center and found the soul totally wrapped up in gauzy white light that shimmers and moves around the soul, giving the soul the healing energy of Divine Love. If a soul lived a particularly violent life or died feeling bereft, they might remain in this state of healing for up to three months after death. I've been allowed to experience this from a soul's perspective, and it truly is a time of rest, repose and relaxation that is incredibly hard to achieve here.

After the soul emerges from this healing cocoon, shamans, mediums and psychics like me will be allowed to interact with the soul and ask for information to pass along to the families and friends still incarnate on Earth. It is at this juncture that souls will take on their younger persona. If there are pictures of souls from his/her twenties and thirties, this is the image or form that I usually see. If the soul was a child when they decided to leave the body, I will see the child at the age of their departure. But for older people in their forties and up, they present to me as their younger, more vibrant, selves.

For example, when my mother died at age forty-seven, I was only twenty-two. Every time I have seen her since in the astral plane, I have seen her as a young woman aged twenty-five to twenty-seven. I once asked my maternal grandmother to show me pictures of my mother at that age, for I had no memory of her that young. I was stunned to see an image that was taken of her at twenty-seven, in the *same* outfit that I had seen her wearing in the astral plane despite the fact that I couldn't recall her in that outfit when she was alive. I later learned that mom borrowed this outfit from a friend during a visit.

It is little situations like this that help mystics and shamans confirm that what we see in the astral plane really is a "truth" and not something in our imagination. I frequently remind my students, when you question the truth of the experiences you are having, ask yourself this question, 'Am I good enough to have thought this up for myself?' I think you will find that the common answer is, 'Nope, I couldn't have made this up, I'm not *that* good.' (Lots of laughter often follows this statement.)

After the soul leaves the initial space of refreshment and renewal, they often wonder how family and friends still on Earth are doing and what needs to be done to bring them to a place of comfort and peace about the soul's departure. That is when family members often feel prompted to ask mystics like me for information. The deceased family member will have been seen, felt, or experienced in some way by family or friends on Earth. The grieving family member will come to me asking what their loved one is trying to tell them.

Frequently this occurs right at the one-year mark, which is often when the incarnate family member is completing their grieving process and the departed soul is checking in to remind them of lessons that are needed. Or the earth-bound beings request could come when they need a reminder of psychic skills or talents, they have that are dormant and need to be embraced and nurtured for progress on their earthly journey.

Many times, the widow or widower will come to me feeling guilty that they have started to date, or have wished to move on with their life, but they don't wish to offend the memory of a departed spouse. These sessions routinely involve encouragement to move on with life, an encouragement that is projected by the departed spouse or loved one. There is usually so much love in the room during these sessions that many tears are shed in memory of good times and in the relief of learning that life continues in all the different phases of existence.

Departed loved ones share with the incarnate family that they, the soul, are happy, at peace, and in a state of pure joy, and that the soul waits for family to follow them when it is their time to cross over. The soul wishes them to live out their lives to the fullest state of their potential before leaving, which might mean that the incarnate spouse needs to find a companion. Or the incarnate one needs to enter a career path that had never been acted upon. Or, my personal favorite, pursuing a hobby or traveling to have experiences they had felt unable to fulfill while serving as the caretaker for an ill partner.

Loved ones on Earth don't always receive what they want, though. Because departed souls might need a transition period when entering the afterlife, I always ask how long a person has been gone when someone wants to reach out to a departed soul. It's not like calling someone up and asking them to pick up a ringing phone. When a mystic reaches out for an incarnate relative or friend, the departed may or may not come. The response to the channeling depends on timing, courtesy and need, as well as what is being asked.

There are times the information our work-a-day mind thinks we need is not at all what our soul knows we need in that moment. I have been a part of sessions where I went into the astral plane to chat with a departed loved one and was told "no." By further questioning the client, I invariably found out that their reasons for wanting the information were not for the best purposes of all the people involved. Such is the careful consideration and love offered by those in the higher frequencies of expression.

Once the soul has checked in with key family and friends, the guide for their journey through the astral and causal worlds comes and asks what they wish to do. Frequently the soul is reminded of the vastness of All-That-Is by being taken to the records of all the lifetimes this soul has lived upon Earth, as well as other planets and universes. A soul is a complex unifying point of experiences, and there are beings that spend their time recording, cataloging and filing away all the experiences a soul has ever had for us to use after death. Some mystics can access these Akashic records for you while you're still living on the planet. This information can be a source of healing and a reminder of your vast levels of experience that you likely have forgot upon being born to Earth.

As the soul moves about the astral plane remembering all that they are and the many lives and beings that the soul has encountered along the journey, the guide will move the soul about until the appropriate frequency is found for the soul to stay in, the soul stays there until it is time to move for the soul's continued evolution, or it becomes time to incarnate again on Earth. The journey is highly customized to fit the particular experiences a soul wishes to have.

Chapter 13:
A Birth of New Souls

W hen people ask me what I do for my spiritual work, I tell them I am a healer of spiritual disease and illness. I leave the physical healing to physicians and the mental & emotional healing to therapists who have the necessary years of training for such work. My work is in the quantum world, the world of spacetime matrices and the creation of our thoughts. In short, the metaphysical realms.

The metaphysical frequencies are all about comfort levels. You are not forced to do anything. You are not forced to become anything. You are not forced into any activity, form or situation. You are invited, encouraged and acknowledged. It is an incredible place to be. I see why so many people who are mystics, psychics, mediums and shamans find it difficult to come back to the work-a-day world that is crowded by details, needs, agendas, appointments and concrete structure when the world they go to for their healing work is the world of the soul which is light, love and acceptance.

I spend most of my time helping other mystics adjust to the 3-D world rather than the world they know to be true in their hearts. The challenging aspect of being a mystic, psychic, shaman or spiritual healer is that you can do so much good in this life and help so many people with their lives, but when it comes to understanding your own life, you must get help. This has been a huge joke with me and other mystics about the ignorance we have about ourselves despite having so much knowledge to assist others.

There is a Nickelback song called "Savin' Me" that has an excellent video regarding this conundrum. In it, a man pushes a woman away from an accident seconds before she would have been crushed to death. After he saves her life, he starts to see numbers above everyone's head that are counting down. He realizes what he is witnessing is the amount of time each person has left before they die. As soon as he grasps this, he quickly walks over to a mirrored surface to see how much time he has left. Alas, he can't see his own timeline, just everyone else's. Such is the nature of many spiritual gifts.

We all have questions we want answered and dreams and desires we want to experience. As we go about living on this planet, we learn how to manifest our dreams, expand our awareness and increase our impact along the way. There are two things in our lives that are certain. At some point we will pay taxes and we will die. Or so the old joke tells us, right?

Being comfortable with death is something that's been part of me my whole life. It is an understanding or perspective that has managed to get me into trouble, but it has also been my greatest strength. Because of the nature of my mother's occupation as a nurse and my father's military service, death is something that was frequently discussed, planned for and joked about. It wasn't taboo to talk about unlike in some families and cultures.

Because of my openness toward this subject, people often ask me questions that they wouldn't ask their own families. The most common one is, "Do you think they are okay?" after they have just lost a loved one, friend, or co-worker to death. It is a valid concern. We are taught when young about God, spirits, ghosts and scary things that go "bump" in the night. It is natural and important to learn more wherever we can.

In the case of understanding death, help can be tricky to find. If our friends are Christians, they will likely try to help by stating that a loved one is "with God," out of pain and in a better place. These well-meaning statements might exacerbate the pain as you search about for some sort of contentment and peace.

After my mom died, God and I had a serious talk. I did the yelling, screaming and demanding, and He sat in silence, listening to my young adult cries and responding with eloquent, beautiful, nada. I sought answers to Life's deeper questions and wanted them ASAP.

The questions were:

Why are humans here on Earth?

Why do we have life and death?

Why is there so much suffering in this world?

Why can't we all just get along?

Why is my heart hurting now that mom is dead and with *You*?

To my young mind, life just didn't make sense, and if there was one thing that I had been taught, it was that God makes sense. That is, if you could get the Big Guy to break His silence with you. At the age of twenty-two, I set myself on a path to learn what this craziness we call "Life" is all about. After spending twenty-five plus years meditating in three different religions and taking umpteen classes on spiritual disciplines while spending hours upon hours in meditation postures, God finally did break His silence with me. When that happened in 2010 such intense love showered over me and erupted from within me that I have built a life focused on teaching others how to gain their version of this experience.

Enlightenment is a target I recommend others walk toward. That's the real challenge of this life path. Once you achieve the ability to talk to God and have God respond to you, you're living in indescribable joy, alongside the challenge of knowing that you can't give this experience to anyone. Every soul must walk their own path back to their Creator.

One of the things that I didn't expect after my initial experience of conversing with God was the amount of souls I would be dealing with and speaking to, both on Earth and in the astral plane. Many people have written about their near-death experiences (NDEs), and I am grateful to each and every one of these writers who have taken the time to record their lives in such a manner. It makes my job as a metaphysician easier. It helps to point to many different accounts from people of all walks of life to demonstrate that life continues after death. Our definitions of ourselves as humans and souls must change from the old, "one-and-done," paradigm that states that when our soul leaves the body, we are dead rather than recognizing the soul's continued growth, and expansion.

My understanding of the regions of heaven and hell have been built on decades of experience moving various souls around the different dimensional spaces as well as the different frequencies of existence. When Christ talks about, "My father's house has many rooms," I can truly respond, "No doubt!" I've experienced so many different aspects to the Divine Realms, yet there is no way in one lifetime on Earth I would learn them all.

So, I keep myself in a need-to-know mindset. This keeps me from ever despairing as a scholar over all the incredible places I wish to visit but just don't have the time or understanding to fully appreciate. Let's just say, I know there is much I don't know and am eager to continue learning and growing in my understanding of Creation.

But let's come back down to earth for a moment. When I have a client come to me asking me to find out about their departed loved one, my first question is; "How long have they been gone?"

The response helps determine for shamans the accessibility of the soul due to the recovery process that occurs after death. Each soul is unique and requires different types of recovery. In my experience a soul often takes three full Earth days to recover from the transitional death experience and to come fully awake in the metaphysical world on the astral plane. There are exceptions to this; Ascended Masters and some of the Native Americans I have worked with come awake almost instantly upon death, and I can communicate with them quite readily because of their knowledge of the metaphysical spaces and the speed of their transition. However, three days seems to be a common starting point for communication with my clients and their passed loved ones.

It was these experiences regarding death, the transition of the soul to certain frequencies, the soul's ability to create a customized heaven or hell, that lead Source to answer one of my philosophical challenges. This experience would change my understanding of what it meant to be a soul.

I had seated myself to meditate one night in 2011 and it took longer than usual to calm my nerves and mind after a rather engaging day of taking care of children, unpacking boxes from our recent move to Columbus, Ohio, and the details of setting up a home in a new city. With all the recent changes going on in my head, I had to do an inordinate amount of breathing techniques to clear the swirling thoughts that kept trying to intrude on my time with Source. After twenty minutes of working on calming myself, I was about to stand back up and just go to bed, when I was riveted to my chair by energy. My entire body stiffened, and I was propelled spiritually into a frequency of thought that I had never been in before.

Spiritually I took note of where I was. It was a space that allowed three-dimensionality in thinking, but there was a "wall" that was a sort of barrier between frequencies. I was supposed to wait on this side of the undulating, fabric like wall. Daddy pushed His face through the barrier just enough for me to see an image so I could focus on Him. He then told me He had a surprise for me. I had always wanted to know where souls came from; He told me that I was about to see the creation process now.

As my soul stood waiting in this metaphysical space for what came next, another being appeared with me. He was the Archangel Metatron (AA Metatron). He stood facing me about four feet away. As we waited, a bulge appeared in the barrier and the shape of a sphere pinched itself off from the barrier and floated between us, right between our feet. I was reminded of the way Golgi bodies, tiny spheres that are created from material inside our body's cells. This process of creation looked similar. As AA Metatron and I continued to observe this creation, Daddy downloaded into my head that this was the process of souls coming from higher dimensional realms and that this was their first experience of being "individualized" away from Source.

These spheres were total and complete Joy. Their excitement at being given an opportunity to be a part of this experience of our universe was "play" to them. They were extremely childlike in their trust, joy, adventurousness and curiosity. They were spheres of energy and light and they were ready to see what was next. As the conga line of spheres bobbed along between AA Metatron's feet and mine, we put our hands out in blessing to each sphere, welcoming them and letting them know there would be guides, resources and support for them throughout their travels. It was almost like they were tourists on this trip, and they couldn't wait to get started on the Ultimate Grand Adventure Tour we humans call Life.

It is hard to describe the sheer joy each of these souls emanated. Their excitement at being given an opportunity to expand and form into whatever beings they wanted to become had them vibrating so strongly that AA Metatron and I were having to frequently remind them to slow their frequencies down or they would pop right back into Source. As I recall this experience, I laugh, because their joy was palatable. Literally, they were like bubbles of laughter. The line of spheres/souls that was coming through into this realm stretched for a long distance. It is hard to comprehend the vastness of the number. Each sphere/soul was irrepressible as it expressed its joy and desires for what it wanted to do first. As I watched the line of souls 'bend' down into the different realms, I observed guides and beings from all over the Universe come to help these souls transition into the various experiences they wished to have.

I returned to my body rather suddenly. Night had fallen hours ago, and I was looking at the full moon shining through my bedroom window. It would take me a few minutes to get my mind and body to work together again. As often occurred after spirit travel to the higher frequencies, when I thought to move a finger, it'd take a count of three for it to happen. There is so much difference in the speed of understanding and knowing on the causal planes versus in our earthly existence.

As I continued to slow my own expectations and harmonize to be-ing a woman on planet Earth with a family, a home and a purpose, I absorbed what I had just participated in. Wow. I got to see the beginning of souls moving into this realm. I was watching a new generation of beings arriving into our universe to experience all that it has to offer. I was beginning to understand why there are some children of this new generation that have difficulty moving within society as it is. No wonder they have trouble sitting still, listening to the slowness of speech.

These souls could process data so quickly that to keep from getting bored they needed to listen to music, while playing a game on their computer while the TV is blaring at them in the background. They literally want to experience as much as possible as soon as possible in the least amount of space as possible.

I began to giggle as I thought of the number of parents, I'd heard accuse their kids of living in their own "bubble" and telling the kids, "That's not how this world works." My understanding of these children that I had remembered would soon attract these souls to my teaching practice.

Chapter 14:
Finding Your Divine Path

◆

After the decades-long search for my Creator through meditation, after hundreds of indescribable experiences, after years of internal psychological training, it was still stressful to receive the vision that I needed to write a series of books. I had written for years on the basic principles of personal money management, math, science, and homeschooling. But I was so *not* a writer of the metaphysical world.

The information that I had been given over twenty-something years had come in the spiritual plane, not through the normal channels of lessons, courses or a scholarly pursuit of a theology degree. I see huge differences in the way spirituality is approached. My personal definition of spirituality is broken down into the approach used by the individual. There are the mystics and then there are the theologians. Mystics have personal experiences with the Divine and get their knowledge from metaphysical experiences. Theologians study the Divine, relying on the written word and knowledge brought about by long hours of committed scholarship.

I found myself being asked to write about a spirituality that had been in-formed by experiences gained from a blend of exposures to multiple countries, cultures, and cannons, so that I couldn't ascribe a single source for my view point. The best I could do when introducing myself was, "Hi, I'm Janine, a recovering Catholic," and go from there. How was I supposed to write a series of books on the Divine? The experiences I had undergone were too far outside of anything I had read or heard about from other people, living or dead. How was I supposed to reveal such an intimate understanding when so much of my training had been to *not* talk about personal things? When I sat in meditation to get inspiration, I was given a simple suggestion. "Janine, just start writing." So, I did.

The biggest aspect of Daddy's realm that I am compelled to share with you is His perspective filtered through my teeny-tiny one. God is too vast and too enigmatic to allow a single soul, like me, to know all there is to know about Him. However, the itty-bitty perspective that I do have may be able to help you along your path in remembering All-That-You-Are. If nothing else, it will give you an example.

The point is this; you *can* communicate directly with your Creator in a loving, peaceful way without the need for external validation from anyone. The way you are living your life is the correct way for you, and if folks don't like it, *too bad*. Your boss is God. Your boss is Source. Your boss is your version of your Creator.

There is so much love and light in the upper realms of Daddy's Creation. I hope that this book has given you a bit of a glimpse into the heaven on earth, and beyond, that can be yours; that it inspires you to go within and learn more about Source for yourself. The questions that originally drove me into learning more about the Divine were:

Why are humans here on Earth? Answered.
Why do we have life and death? Answered.
Why is there so much suffering in this world? Answered.
Why can't we all just get along? Answered.
Why does my heart hurt now that mom is dead and with *You* (God)? Answered.

My hope now is to inspire you to connect with your own soul and remember that you, too, have answers to your life queries. Any question, no matter how complicated, convoluted or contorted will be answered by your connection with your Source.

So, how do you do this? Well, from all my life experiences, and having spoken to hundreds of mystics, healers, psychics and scholars, I have found a few methods that work; meditation, self-analysis, and journaling.

Chapter 15:
Sitting in Silence

◆

c

Not that long ago, if you mentioned that you meditated, the first image that would pop into most people's minds was one of a thin Asian man sitting cross-legged on the ground with his wrists resting on his knees, hands uplifted, chanting "Om" for hours. This stereotype persisted for many Americans long after the '60s brought us the Peace Movement, Hippies, free love and LSD.

Back then, meditation was for folks with long hair who smoked marijuana and didn't bother bathing. However, after Woodstock, the Peace Movement went mainstream, and alternative lifestyle choices other than those glamorized during the '50s were embraced. And then there was the invasion of Tibet. How are these events connected? When the Dali Lama had to remove himself from his mountain retreat in Tibet, breaking a 317-year lineage of tradition, it also opened up exposure to meditation practices. Since that time and the revolution of thinking that the '60s brought America, we've had a huge influx of spiritually based meditation practices brought to us from India, Japan, and China.

Meditation is now practiced as a form of healing and is being prescribed as a therapeutic method by Western medicine. As yoga and spirituality became more popular, partly due to teachers brought here and through international travel, then the '70s and '80s helped people operate more from a globally aware spiritual perspective. Then the Internet gave us a huge leap in connectivity, allowing us to share the different perspectives of what makes us human more freely, and inspiring more people to share their understandings.

This globalization of spiritual knowledge has helped meditation be embraced as a way to keep your balance in a life of change. In a world that seems to want to throw us into a state of chaos, it is good to have a process to harmonize our focus when there is so much clamoring for attention. We are inundated with so much input from our senses as well as our devices. Over the past several decades, I have coached hundreds of mystics with spiritual gifts that ranged in ability and strength, no matter how gifted each was, they all needed time to "check in" and ground through their meditation practice and "check out" of what the world calls reality for a short time each day. The form of meditation, the system of meditation and the experiences received through meditation varied, but the process is the same.

Our souls are in a human avatar, to borrow the term from video games. We move about this planet operating at a fraction of our capabilities and true nature. We are all so much more than can be expressed through our human frame. Even while we deal with reality through our six senses (hearing, seeing, smelling, tasting, touch, and ESP) we can stay quite connected to Source. Meditation is a daily reminder to remain in harmony, to anchor yourself in an internal place of peace, despite living a 3-D, detail-oriented life. Meditation reminds us to have fun within life and is the key to mastering unhelpful perceptions of life.

Due to spending umpteen hours in meditation and the many ways I have practiced and studied it, I've had friends jokingly call me a Master Meditator. I would always laugh along, but in my mind, I knew myself as a novice. If all my experiences have taught me anything, it would be, what I have integrated most is just how much I don't know.

There is so much in Creation to learn, experience and become. Meditation has taught many a human how to truly help people. Spiritual gifts and knowledge have been downloaded into thousands of people's lives by their daily practice of meditation.

I encourage you to start some sort of habit where you sit in silence. Notice, I didn't say sit in prayer. Why? Because prayer is you talking to God. Meditation is listening for the answers. You are barraged every day by information and stimulation. Many folks just want to move into a stress-free state and wish they could remember how to relax. Sleeping is not enough to relax, because once you wake up, your mind starts spinning and, literally, your thoughts pick up where you left off the day before. It is time to stop the cycle of stress that you have accepted as being life. I encourage you to start expanding your ability to rest and relax through meditation. It is the primary cure-all that aids our body's ability to heal from physical, emotional, mental and spiritual challenges. Just as Tylenol helps physical pain, so meditation heals emotional, mental, and spiritual pain.

So, how do you go about this meditation gig? What can you focus on for this process to work in your favor? Do you have to sit for hours like I did to achieve epic results? Nope. But you do have to sit. When students have told me that meditation simply doesn't work for them, I break down the different systems of meditation and then we work on building a custom process for their particular lifestyle.

However, no matter what background you have in meditation, and whether you are a seasoned mediator or not, I know a system you can implement to get really good at this practice.

To meditate, a few things are required to achieve epic results.

The basics are:

1. Get your calendar and figure out what time each day you can sit down for three minutes to meditate. That's it! Just three minutes.

2. After you've decided on a time of day, decide *where* you are going to meditate.

3. Then, set an alarm or notification on your phone to alert you that it is time to meditate.

4. To test out this approach, before you go to bed today, sit down for three minutes and do nothing. I mean, not *anything*. Just sit there.

Feel what it is like to sit and do absolutely nothing for three minutes.

Now, many of my clients have told me that this feels like punishment. The last time they sat and did nothing was when they were young children, and an adult was reprimanding them. Please remember that you are now sitting in silence as a gift to yourself, to give yourself some rest and deep relaxation. You are giving yourself permission to reconnect with All-That-You-Are, the Divine that is within you.

Much of who we are gets forgotten about due to the way we live life. Meditation is a process to use for remembering (and for connecting to Source, whether you become consciously aware of this connection or not). One way to help yourself take meditation more seriously is to write a contract to yourself about meditating. Below is a sample for you to use if you want.

My Meditation Permission Slip

I, _____ (insert your name) give myself permission to sit quietly each day for at least 3 Minutes in a state of rest and relaxation.

I allow myself to have this time, knowing that it will help my body, mind, and soul to be in connection with my Higher Power.

I will do my best to release any guilt that may arise for giving myself this quiet time. I do not speak silently or aloud any word to berate or punish myself for giving myself this time of peace.

Just as I know that, in an emergency on an airplane, I must first put my oxygen mask on myself before I can effectively help others around me, so too must I have this quiet, peaceful time with my guides, guardians, the heavenly realm, and Creator to be of service to people in my life and humanity at large.

_____   _____

Signature   Date

Chapter 16:
Finding Spirit in Silence

◆

Okay, now that you have given yourself permission to sit in silence, it is time for you to remind yourself how to be an active listener for the answers that will come into your understanding. Many, many times during meditation I wouldn't feel like anything was happening. I can remember one especially dark time where it felt like I had lost all the empathic and psychic gifts I had enjoyed for fifteen years. They were just gone, poof! I sat in total darkness and would cry out into that darkness. Nothing. Despite the lack of response, despite the deafening quiet, despite the feelings of abandonment, I continued to meditate each day. I'm stubborn like that.

My thought process was one of a two-year-old. It went something like this, "Fine, if you're not going to speak to me and take all my gifts back, fine! I'm going to sit here and scream at you until you answer me." I plopped myself into my meditation chair every day for six months of darkness. Life continued and then one day, quite suddenly, I plopped down into my meditation chair for another session of darkness when a gentle stirring in my soul was felt. It was so shocking to my expectation to have nothing happen that I stated out loud, "Hello?" The answer was the memory of a story that I had read twenty years earlier.

The story was of a vision that St. Therese of Lisieux, known as the Little Flower, stated in one of the many books I had read on saints. She summarized her vision as a "time of darkness for six months" where Jesus had removed from her any ability to see, feel or hear him. She had prayed and meditated on the Divine just as much, if not more, than I had, and she was having this similar experience. Later in recounting her experience, she explained that Christ did return to her; that she had experienced the shadow of darkness because he was stretching out His hand to her. In that process of Him reaching out, a shadow is formed that proceeds the Divine's Touch.

After remembering this story, I felt the Divine Touch gently stroke my soul. No words were used. No telepathic messages, but the purest love I had ever experienced in my life. A deep compassion that I was not lost, I was not separated from Daddy, I was not being punished, as He reached out to touch me, the shadow had been cast upon me by His coming. This was a lesson so intense and yet so beautiful that all I could do was put my head in my hands and cry at the startling, crystal-clear love and purity of the relationship I was experiencing in that moment. As quickly as it came, the feeling vanished. I instantly stopped the flow of tears and I was sitting in my meditation chair. However, rather than feeling any darkness, I felt a sense of completion.

My empathic and psychic gifts had returned, and I was stronger than I remember being before. It was like in all the hero movies that have been released by Marvel. At some point the hero loses his special powers, mechanical suit or physical talents for a period of time. What does the hero do? He keeps on doing what he can with the elements of himself that remain. Like me, he just kept meditating. Then when the hero's talents return - boom, he can do more, he is stronger, and he has a whole new format to use in his life. Well, I was feeling like the feminine version of all the comic books heroes I had followed as a child.

After this experience, I started researching the saints and sages from as many religions I could, and I began to find how each one had experienced the darkness much like I had. Many of the meditative mystics or the prayerful sages described periods of their practices in which the only thing that kept them going was the practice itself. The *habit* of doing the practice, of staying in connection with self no matter what, saw them through the darkness so that they could have more amazing connections once they made it through the darkness.

I share this with you to help you with the beginning of meditation. When you first start the habit of sitting in silence it is easy to become fidgety and frustrated. I will have folks who have meditated for a month or less tell me, "Nothing is happening, I see nothing. I experience nothing. All I see is black." My response is a simple, "How do you know nothing is happening?" Spending only a month listening in silence is hardly the darkness that I was describing before. When you first start meditating you have to get into the habit of not being entertained. You have to get into the experience of doing nothing. You get to feel what it is like to spend time with just you and listening to just you.

Now, the question is, how well do you like yourself? This can be a major stumbling block for some people. As you sit in silence your mind will want to wander and dance around. There will be a zillion thoughts that will race through your head reminding you of the multiple details of your current life. People, events, memories, to-do lists, groceries, bills and the entirety of your panoramic life will scroll through your mind's eye as you sit. There is a way to calm this sea of details and thoughts.

Remember that the mind cannot control the mind. It must be done through a different method. This is where you use your body to control your mind. Cool, no?

As you sit to meditate for your three minutes, the moment you settle into a comfortable seated position, it is important to set up a routine for yourself. I am going to suggest a routine below for you to begin with; feel free to expand on the time and techniques as you learn more about yourself.

My Meditation Routine

1. Sit as comfortably as your body will let you.

2. Set some sort of intention for your meditation; say a prayer, or focus on a calming image.

3. Take a deep inhale through your nose and hold for two to three seconds, and then breathe out through your mouth with a "huh-huh" sound. Do this two more times. You will find your mind calmer and slower than when you first sat to meditate.

4. Gently roll your closed eyes up without strain as you breathe naturally. Just let your eyes rest while looking up. This keeps your focus in the super conscious mind rather than looking straight ahead, where you're more likely to keep a focus on the details of day-to-day living.

5. Sit and pay attention to your breath. This sounds silly but it is a technique that has been taught for thousands of years. You are keeping your mind busy by closing your eyes and gently rolling them up, and you are staying physically engaged with your body by feeling your breath moving in and out of your chest.

6. Feel the coolness of the breath moving into your body and the heat of the breath moving out of your body.

7. Allow yourself permission to sit and only focus on your breathing with your eyes gently looking up. Do this for three minutes. Ta da! You are a meditator.

Chapter 17:
Finding the Ultimate Joy

◆

When you first start meditating, you'll think there isn't much happening. But as you continue resting with yourself in the silence, you will start to notice little things throughout the day that will positively affect you. This is born from your meditative practice. Three minutes a day is powerful, although the shifts occurring in you can start off quite subtly and then build over time. This process is akin to anything requiring daily attention. It depends on what kind of life you wish to live. If you're happy with where you are and you are settled into a life that brings you contentment and peace, then meditation will allow you to express that joy to others by magnifying it.

If you wish to change your life to bring about greater creativity, beauty and more inspiration for new ways to expand your knowledge base, perspective or manifested skills, meditation allows you to calm your mind and heart so that you give yourself space to receive the intuitive flow that operates within you. I call this the "more and better" mindset where I encourage people not to worry about changing unless they want to become more or better.

If you feel that your life is in chaos and you're seeking stability and answers to the deeper philosophical questions that you have, meditation calms your physical responses so that your spiritual guidance can come through. It is hard to hear your intuition when your mind and heart are in a swirling mass of thoughts and conflicting emotions.

The biggest lesson I received as I learned about the creation of souls and the spiritual realms was that each soul on this planet wants to be here to ride *the Ride of the Universe.* That ride is our earthly life. We are on this planet to have fun. We made a choice to experience the ups and downs of emotions, the excitement of ideas, the successes of achieving goals, the lessons in failures. There is so much on this planet to enjoy, learn, and interact with. So, if, you make the assumption that we are supposed to have fun, why don't we? Well, that's where the finger pointing, and excuses come in.

During my life, I have realized that when I really think about why I'm not happy, there is only one person I can point the finger to…

That would be me.

There was a period of time after my enlightenment in which I really examined my desire to be happy. I would sit in meditation for an hour a day, seeking to know why I wasn't as happy as I had been in the spiritual world. I had been doing so much healing work for others, and I was finding that I was beginning to lose my joy and my thrill of living on this planet. I was starting to notice my thoughts were withdrawing from crowds and large gatherings. This is a natural cycle for anyone who works in the shamanistic or spiritual fields, but instead of just shrugging it off or accepting it as normal, I really studied my emotions and the thoughts that would pop up as I found myself pulled by the appeal of an introverted life.

It was during this thirty days that I came to understand the true power I had to "create my reality." I had heard this statement over and over, but I had never truly integrated it with experiences I had lived through. However, the more I studied the deep need I was now experiencing for bringing joy into my day-to-day life the more my mind stumbled across fallacies that I had taken as fact in the way this world and this reality worked. I learned that I had ideas and concepts that were no longer true for me.

The three biggest fallacies I had accepted as my truth were:

1. I blamed others for my emotions.
2. I argued *for* my misery or discontent.
3. I created anger as a way to stay out of depression.

These false perspectives on life were extremely uncomfortable to challenge. There was a part of my ego that didn't want to address the errors in my thinking. Ego wanted me to get up out of my meditation chair and "do something, anything, *now!*" rather than examine the faulty logic that was keeping me in a place of mental stagnation. As I looked at these three concepts that were errors in my programming, I came to understand that Daddy was showing me where I needed to change so that I could fully integrate the mission I was to manifest in my life. I would not be able to achieve my highest potential if I continued to live with these three errors running my life from the depths of my subconscious mind. Now that I could "see" these errors in my thinking, it was time to address them.

As I examined each error, startling realizations of my upbringing, my culture, my nationalism, and my family began bubbling up in my mind.

I was shown memory after memory of life experiences that had led to my erroneous conclusions of how I was to operate on this planet in order to remain safe. But these thoughts, they had no longer served me. So, with no fanfare, no celebration, no event planning, I slowly and methodically picked away at each error until I removed it from my processing of life.

How did I do this? Let's look at each error.

The first one, "I blame others for my emotions," came from early childhood training when I was told by family and friends "not to hurt others' feelings." Anytime my blunt and tactless observations were stated out loud (I was apparently "too honest") about the world I saw, I was reprimanded for not being more aware and for hurting other people's feelings. This training set up an error in my thinking that I had control over others' feelings, and they had control over mine. This was the largest problem I was currently facing in my life. I was wide open to the world now after my enlightenment experiences. I was fully in my power and I knew exactly who I was and why I was on the planet.

My current struggle was to integrate all the lessons I had learned in the spiritual realms and express them in my daily life. Believing that I was not the one in control of my emotions interfered with that integration of My Truth. I specify this as My Truth because each mystic will discover their own Truth through meditation and enlightenment experiences. By sharing My Truth, I hope to help you in learning yours.

The second error I had was that "I argued for my misery and discontent." As I observed the way I interacted with the people, conversations and events around me, I observed how others and myself would argue for our limitations, our low pay, our awful jobs, our bad health and our small view of ourselves. I learned to spot in my own words where I was arguing for the right to be miserable in my life. I would state certain life events, recount old experiences and draw upon childhood trauma to be my guide on why I had to remain a certain way. Or I would limit myself in my full expression of who I truly was. This had to stop. As I paid more attention to my day-to-day conversations, I watched the words that came out of my mouth. I purposely slowed my speech down and made sure that what I was saying about myself, my life, my experiences and those around me didn't contradict the life experiences I really wanted.

The third error in my thought processes was, "I created anger to stay out of depression," proved the hardest one to examine.

My programming had been that I was the one responsible for others' anger towards me. I was so used to internalizing anger. As I woke up to who I really was, I came to understand that my anger at others was hiding a deep depression. And in order for me to keep from falling into the void of despair, I used anger and blame to keep me going when all I really wanted to do was curl up in a ball under the bed covers and tell the world to "go away."

I realized that any time I got angry, one of two things was going on. One, I was expecting a result that I really wanted, and it didn't happen the way I wanted it to occur, so I was super disappointed. Then, as more stuff occurred in my life to thwart my desired outcome, I would move down the scale of emotions from disappointment to discontent to irritation to anger. If I allowed myself to drop down below anger, I would land in the gray world of depression and inaction. I couldn't allow myself to do that, so I would express anger.

Another reason I became angry was a lack of faith. That was a tough pill for me to swallow when I realized this. After everything I had been through, anger was my way of stating that I didn't think I was going to get what I wanted out of life. Really? I looked at that belief in disbelief when I saw it for the raw expression that this error was presenting. I immediately took steps to remove this error from my processing modes in my mind. This error was from generations of my family lineage living hand-to-mouth, from a scarcity mentality that didn't apply to my current existence. It, too, was going to have to leave my processing.

As I continued to meditate, observe, and remove thoughts and incorrect beliefs over several years, my mindset and life went from confusion and fogginess to crystal clear clarity. I saw my path before me, and I knew what I had to do with my life. I wasn't going to take "no" for an answer. I was done living from fallback behavior and in fear. I was going to move forward with the life I knew I needed to live and go about making plans and goals for what I needed to accomplish. This new commitment to myself had radically altered my understanding of the people, events, and perspectives around me. I saw my life and conversations with new clarity. As I reviewed my life and saw it for how it truly had manifested rather than from the fogginess of not knowing what parts of my behavior were due to me, I was stunned by the corner I had painted myself into.

I wasn't happy with where I was. It wasn't healthy for me, my children, husband, family, or friends. No wonder I battled anger all the time. My life needed an overhaul. So that is what I did.

I will talk about the changes I made in greater depth in the next volume for now, let's focus on getting you to your pure potential. Let's see about getting you into a meditation practice, or, if you're already meditating, let's see if you can remember even more about your particular soul's journey.

Chapter 18:

Serving Through Your Divine Connection

◆

I cannot stress enough how important it is that you meditate and decide to make the necessary changes in life to be happy. As I learned more and more about myself and what I needed to do to bring my life experience into one of joy and delight, I realized all the hundreds of ways that I kept myself out of joy by the inaccurate teachings I had assimilated as I walked through life.

We have over seven billion people on Earth, all seven billion of whom are living lives according to their own dictates and creativity. There are millions of ways to live life. If you are not happy with where you are in life and what it looks like, then it is time to do something about it. Go sit down! Be still. Calm your thoughts and your breathing. Listen to the wisdom of your Higher Self. You are a smart person!

How do I know? You've read this entire book looking for answers to your own life journey. I know that you have your own answers within your soul. Go to the one place where you hear yourself clearly. That is in meditation. By focusing on goals that will bring experiences into your life that you wish to live, by meditating so that you can hear your own intuition guiding you along your life path, you will find yourself attracted to the very people, books and resources that can help you get the life experiences you seek. The process will bring joy and laughter back into your life. The question is, are you willing to listen to your own, good advice? This is the gift of meditation.

If you already have a form of meditation that you use, go deeper into your practice. Commit now to bringing yourself to a higher understanding of yourself and what your practice is doing for you. If you need a refresher course, take one. The point is, for seasoned, veteran meditating souls, your efforts to raise your vibration to pure potential, or to harmonize with your Creator, sends out positive vibratory effects like ripples on a pond. Your meditative practice produces calming, loving waves of light and has a major impact on the people who know you. It helps them and, in return, helps you connect to Source in a stronger, more conscious way.

I offer on-line classes in meditation. If you are interested in learning the different forms, systems and styles of meditation or wish to get a different perspective on the style of meditation you use, feel free to sign up for a six-week course that I offer. (www.the8gates.com)

You make a strong difference in this world by being harmonized with your highest spiritual goals and then manifesting those goals in your life. You become a huge beacon of light and you change the world just by living in it and making daily decisions that offer understanding rather than judgment, compassion rather than anger, joy rather than negativity. Keep doing your best to bring the good you wish to experience into this world through your own life's activities. The ripple effect is huge.

I see this effect frequently in my own meditations. When I meditate, I float above this planet and am given a beautiful view. The first time Source showed me the number of souls incarnated on this planet as a whole, I was stunned. Imagine seeing seven billion individual specks of Light. It was blinding, but slowly my eyes adjusted to the experience and I was able to discern individual beings. Then the scene changed, and I was shown that there are individual beings that live on the planet that have totally cleared their karma. They came into a body to live life and make the world a better place one person at a time. They don't have karma to burn. They aren't here to "learn" life lessons and they didn't need to clear any gunk from past lives. These souls volunteered to come to this planet and have a great time living, working and loving. They came here to enjoy the ride that their multi-dimensional soul could have in a small, limited, avatar we call a 3-D human body.

You are one of these souls in the process of rediscovering yourself. How do I know? Because you wouldn't have been drawn to read this book otherwise. I wrote this book for specific souls who live on this planet and may be feeling a bit punch drunk from all the events that have happened to them. I wrote this book to reach out to the souls that I see in my meditations as small points of Light who are making the world a better place just by living in it with their compassion, care and concern for others.

You *are* making a difference every day. I see the light and I can feel the increase in harmony. Thank you for being here on this planet.

Scientific studies have shown that the amount of violence on this planet has gone down. Just remember that when you are watching the news and you walk away with the impression that violence is on the rise; keep in mind that these activities are only seen as newsworthy because they are rare relative to the normal day-to-day news that underlies most local, national and international activities.

Keep meditating. Bring peace into your life. Learn to live your life with every thought, every decision and every action dedicated to your living a happy life. Your personal joy is the greatest gift you can give this planet, this community, this family, this moment, this you.

Chapter 19:
And One More Thing...

◆

When I first set about writing a three-volume set on the experiences I had while seeking, finding and expressing the Divine, my intention was to demonstrate to others how possible it is to find your own answers to your life. I wanted you to know that you make good choices when it comes to how you live as long as you keep in the forefront of your mind the need your soul has for expressing joy. Now, I realize that to run around every day all day in a total state of joy is not probable since even babies and small children express displeasure when they get uncomfortable. So the point is to bring about the deeper joy of a clear mind and a happy disposition that is the natural state of being for the soul. That state has been forgotten because of the trainings you've received from well-meaning family and friends. More of this will be covered in greater detail in the next book.

As a scientist I can tell you that just because someone thinks the world works in a specific way, doesn't mean that "way" is right for you. If you are unhappy with your life right now, I highly recommend that you start meditating on a regular basis. Meditate on calming your thoughts and resting in the company that is you. When was the last time you just spent time with only you? No media. No books. No person speaking to you. When was the last time that you just sat with your own thoughts, listened to your breath and calmed yourself by focusing on you? Just three minutes a day will do! Get started on this habit and you'll see your life change for the better.

If you already meditate, make sure you start being consistent in your practice. You affect the world in ways you may not see right now, but shamans and mystics like me notice the difference as we move about the planet. We can feel spots in neighborhoods, grocery stores and at events that have had folks walking around whose simple presence sends out blessings to all that result from their interior practice and prayer.

Lastly, for those of you who meditate daily and would label yourselves consistent in your practice, you know who you are. You've been meditating for decades and have gone through multiple systems and trainings. You're the type that is ever working deeper and deeper to think differently about situations so that you receive positive results. Your attitude to your life situations and the systematic handling of your life have people in awe of your calmness.

Keep on meditating and set goals for your practice that are in line with your training. You are serving the world and helping others at a high level by this form of "spiritual selfishness."

I encourage you to continue to be selfish and spend as much time as you need in meditation while you continue to pay bills, meet people, tidy your home, run errands, do laundry, travel and keep your life moving in the direction you wish it to go.

The next volume in this series is *Expressing the Divine*.

In it I will cover the tools and systems I use to manifest what I know into the life I live as well as bring to you the lives and experiences of the many saints, sages and mystics that I have had the honor to meet, work with and learn from.

It is my hope that this series will inspire you in your own spiritual practice while demonstrating to you the many paths to experiencing a state of bliss and joy that never leaves you.

It is a practice that keeps you walking the road of life in a harmonized way.

I hope to hear from you soon.

Contact me at www.the8gates.com or

Drop me an email at Janine@the8gates.com

Annotated Bibliography

H ere are some books that have helped me greatly in my spiritual journey. These tomes will not be able to replace meditation for developing personal experiences with Source, but they offer reassurance that you are not alone on your path. Many types of mystics have been successful at self-discovery even in the face of major challenges. These are the inspirational books that helped me stay on track:

The 7 Habits of Highly Effective Teens, Sean Covey. This is the best book in the world for practical tips on changing the way you live. Goal setting, humor and cartoons are all included in one book. Excellent for keeping you on track to where you wish to go. This book is way better than his dad's original, *7 Habits of Highly Effective People,* written years before. Every student I've ever taught had to read this book. It is that important to life success. I've read it over 14 times in the past two decades since its release.

Ask and It is Given, Esther and Jerry Hicks. If you enjoy a book that teaches and then gives you honest-to-goodness practice steps, this is for you. When I read this book in 2015, I loved how the exercises walked you through different types of systems for thinking through your self-limiting beliefs and emotions. There are over twenty-two different systems to choose from for making your life better.

Autobiography of a Yogi, Paramahansa Yogananda. This landmark book got me into a spiritual form of discipline that would last the rest of my life.

Not everyone is as single-minded as I am when it comes to goal setting, but Yogananda's experiences with his awakening are eloquently described, giving you another example of what it means to engage in life and still keep a quietness of mind amidst chaos.

How We Die: Reflections on Life's Final Chapter, Sherwin B. Nuland. I read this book in 1995 when I was doing a lot of coaching on going through grief. It was a great reminder that we will all die, and it is up to us to figure out what that needs to look like. After considering the way my mom died, I was better able to make choices on how I wanted to die after reading this book. The latest edition has an added chapter on the current practices in health care and ways that you might want your family to work with you should you develop a terminal illness or one of the seven major diseases that can be terminal. Yes, the book was written twenty years ago, but not much has changed in the process of dying, only the amount of control patients now have in their care.

The Law of Attraction: The Basics of the Teachings of Abraham, Esther and Jerry Hicks. I didn't read this book until 2014 when a friend gave it to me and told me much of what I was teaching was also in this book. Well, let's just say I devoured this book as the authors explain, in clear, concise secular language, a spiritual path devoid of religious entanglements and the practice of the path involved. A wonderful book!

Life in the World Unseen, Anthony Borgia. This book is a pleasant perspective of the afterlife as experienced by Monsignor Robert Hugh Benson. He shared his perspective with Borgia after he died. Benson's belief that he and the other souls he sees will continue their spiritual evolution for all eternity in the afterlife realm is in contradiction to my own life experiences with reincarnation, but that does not negate this book or the poetic mind of Monsignor Benson. For people who are just learning about the afterlife, I recommend this as a solid starting point.

The Power of Myth, Joseph Campbell. Campbell experienced enlightenment at the age of 27 and spent the rest of his life using academic scholarship and lectures to teach what he knew. He was brilliant at integrating the stories and legends of tribal peoples all over the world and using their metaphors to create purposeful stories for his readers, students and community. This book helped me incorporate the Greek, Roman, and Hindu perspectives into my Christian metaphors as I moved along my spiritual path. Campbell also helped me overcome the frustrations of fitting language to transcendent experiences.

Glossary of Terms Janine Uses

◆

Below are all the words my students, beta readers and editors ask me to describe in better detail. This is a common problem with modern English. There are so many terms we have borrowed from other languages or customs that the way I use a word may not be the same as you use it. Here are the meanings I have for the following words:

Catechism, *a summary of the principles of Christian religion in the form of questions and answers, used for the instruction of Christians.* Before I was given confirmation and my first communion, I had to attend months of classes with the nuns learning the prayers, questions, and answers of the Roman Catholic Church.

Compassion, *concern for the sufferings and misfortunes of others.* I encourage most people to operate with a sense of compassion toward others rather than empathy. I teach health care professionals the difference between sympathy, empathy and compassion so that they can remain in a state of compassion without becoming burdened in the lower emotional states of sympathy and empathy. As spiritual beings experiencing the range of emotions of human life, it behooves us to stay connected to others through our compassion, but not allow our own emotions to be triggered or involved in a person's suffering. We cannot offer the greatest help to them if we don't vibrate at a higher rate while they are in a vibration of pain. By offering our higher frequency to merge with their frequency, we remind the soul of where they will feel better. It is important as a healer of any kind, to remind the souls that come to us for help that their origin is of a higher vibration, and that our duty as their consultant, mystic or healer, is to remind them of their own power to heal themselves. We offer suggestions on systems, resources, and techniques, but the healing is their own responsibility of listening to their higher guidance for the soul knows how to heal the body.

Diksha, *the laying on of hands by a guru in blessing, the transfer of spiritual gifts or spiritual dispensation.* This is a ceremonial blessing that has been used for centuries in many different countries. I first experienced it in a Hindu Temple in Colorado by Sai Maa before my diksha by Christ.

Empathy, *the ability to feel what another person is feeling.* Most of my life I was taught that empathy was the ability to understand what another was feeling. I have since changed my personal definition. There are people on this planet that totally have the ability to literally feel other people's emotions. They often get confused on "what is mine and what is theirs" as they grow up around others. This confusion is what causes some empaths to become introverts or people-pleasers in an effort to feel better. Empaths will often do whatever they can to help others feel better. Most of our medical professionals are empaths. There are techniques that a person can use to define when an emotion is their own or someone else's.

Grandfather of the West, *a spiritual guide in many Native American traditions who is the keeper of time, the guardian of ancient wisdom and gatekeeper of spiritual gifts. He is the primary teacher to Sacred Clowns and assists shamans with healings in ceremonies.* Grandfather of the West is a metaphor I have seen in many religions as the entity of Death, but it doesn't necessarily mean a physical death. I came to learn that he also represented Bat Medicine (think Plato's cave) of certain shamans who would undergo a spiritual death ceremony as they came into their psychic gifts as healers and mediums.

Sympathy, *feelings of pity or sorrow for someone else's misfortune.* This situation or emotion is a conditioned response we have for others. It is the first step in offering understanding to those around us. We are taught from a young age, that if someone tells us something awful has happened to them, loss of job, death in the family, divorce or natural disaster, we are to offer them condolences if we have no other means of assistance.

A Page for Personal Notes

(I write in books when I read them, I wanted you to have some pages to record your thoughts too!)

CPSIA information can be obtained
at www.ICGtesting.com
Printed in the USA
BVHW081426300819
557242BV00001B/253/P

9 780359 478644